Praise for Helen Burke:

'Helen falls up to the moon, turns the world upside down. Her dreams have no edges. She can conjure up a "lovely glorious carefree hope-filled now" … her memories of childhood, her love of family and people dance in the rhythm of her poetry. She is without guile, witty, truthful, visionary and incisive. She lifts up my spirits, takes me on a star-spattered journey.'
— Norah Hanson

'Helen Burke's non-conformist poems engage the simplicity of natural language in original narratives that convey a highly personal cosmology, and negotiate unexplored spaces of imagination. The poet's complex perception of the world reveals an often extravagant spirit that repudiates stereotypes and clichés, and proposes a fresh approach to understanding life and its meaning.'
— Elena Nistor

'Helen Burke's poems are webs created from a clear, strong voice, threading sadness and humour, ardour and sass, whimsy and wisdom. Life – real and imagined – is exalted so that no matter how you enter Helen's webs, your wings are repaired and your heart is lifted.'
— Emily Davis Fletcher

'Helen Burke's poetry is laced with a delicious spiky humour. She weaves her words slant, with wit, freshness, and constant surprise. The humour is layered over deeper concerns, with mortality and social identity – but the touch is light, wildly imaginative and intensely enjoyable.'
— Chris North

'Helen's poems range from the hilarious to the deeply moving. They offer glimpses of life in all its richness and quirkiness, with arresting images and deft turns of phrase that remain with you. I love them.'
— Gwen Berwick

'When I read Helen Burke's poetry I am beamed into a place where the spirits of Emily Dickinson, every dog in the world, and unnamed fairies speak through Helen's singular voice; with life's dark realities and the wildness of fate.'
— Mary Mueller

'Helen Burke is a poet of multiple enchantments. She has a kaleidoscope eye; little is untouched by her imagination. Burke hides nothing from us; we watch her paint essences with words, conjure menageries that become worlds. Her conversational rhythms catch your ear, then your heart. She trusts us with her pain and feels ours. Assuring us, in "The Flying Suit"; "I sleep fully-clothed in case you should need me". We do.'
— Mary Ann Meyer

'Helen Burke's poems uncover delight in the rarest of places. She understands how words transform the mind and heart into a state of joyful expectation.'
— Jan Keough

'Helen Burke is a lover of language, of life, and of humanity. Anyone remotely interested in any of these things will find so much to discover in her wonderful poems.'
— Giuseppe Albano

'Helen Burke's poetry is a richly-layered tapestry of imagery that leaves you casting anchors on the page to catch breath. She is feisty and fearless, yet vulnerable. Her characters, especially her family, take on heroic proportions. Her poems are humorous, poignant and full of the rich indignity of being alive. In Helen's own words, her poetry is like riding the hobby horse clean off the carousel.'
— Bill Carpenter

Today the Birds Will Sing

Collected Poems 1969 – 2016

POETRY & ILLUSTRATIONS BY
Helen Burke

EDITED BY
Jamie McGarry

Valley Press

First published in 2017 by Valley Press
Woodend, The Crescent, Scarborough, YO11 2PW
www.valleypressuk.com

First edition, first printing (June 2017)

ISBN 978-1-908853-69-1
Cat. no. VP0086

Poems, photographs and illustrations © Helen Burke 2017
Editorial and design content © Jamie McGarry 2017

The right of Helen Burke to be identified as the
author of this work has been asserted in accordance with
the Copyright, Designs and Patents Act 1988.

All rights reserved. No part of this publication may be
reproduced, stored in or introduced into a retrieval system,
or transmitted in any form, by any means (electronic,
mechanical, photocopying, recording or otherwise) without
prior written permission from the rights holders.

A CIP record for this book is available from the British Library.

Printed and bound in Great Britain by
Imprint Digital, Upton Pyne, Exeter.

Contents

THE GARDEN (1969)
Love is the Feeling Between
   Now and Now   17
The Skyline   18
The Lens of the Camera   18

A GAME OF TWO
   HALVES (1979)
Welcome   19
Piano   19
Heart   20
Poem for Mrs Waters   21
Batsi, Andros   22
Foreigner   23
In May   24
Lacing Boots   25
The Film   26
The Aunts   28
Windmills   29
Sun   30
The Prepared Room   31
At Highfield   32
At Elvington   33

LEROS: ISLAND OF
   DREAMS (1994)
Arrival – Leros   34
Here – Now   34
Wing   35
Ankle-Deep   36
Swallows at Aghia   37
Aghia Marina   38
Alinda Bay   39
At the Castle   40

V.E. Day   41
Dawn   41
The Traveller   42
Villa   43
Saint George's Chapel   44
For Bob (in Leros)   44
At Garbo's   45
Patmos   46
Papa Retsina   46
Leros Cat-Walk   47
Vortex   48
Departure   48
Kallinichta   49

POETRY (1995)
Tigers   50
New Girl at the Shop   51
Map   52
Fireworks   54
Space   55
Walkers   56
The Op   57
Sheep   58
Fever Flowers   59
The Flying Suit   60
George   61
Oz   62
Leaving   63
Another Song   64
Aldeburgh   65
On Coats   66
Whale   68

MIDNIGHT IN THE
MORNING (1998)
Hope Street 69
Therapy 70
Mellow Yellow 72
Foxglove 73
Snake 74
India 75
The City 76
Sea-Largo 77
Irish Funeral 78
Gargunnock 79
Boatman 80

FROM THE BOOK OF
BEYOND (2001)
Recipe for a Poet 81
The Happening 83
Billy 85
Second-hand Men 86
Home Town 87
Lazarus Enrolls at the Gym 88
The Back of Beyond 90
The Test 91
Enlightenment 92
Timothy 93
Town People on a Beach 95
Silver Wedding 96
Good Advice 97
Neil, Honey 98
Making Ends Meet 99
The Dog in the Painting 100
Sundays 101
Message 102

ZUZU'S PETALS (2007)
The Chocolate Girls 103
Children's Games 104
When Dad was Father
    Christmas 106
The Apple House 108
Head 110
Strange Meeting 112
The Space Around 113
The Blue Cooker 114
Children's Hospice 116
The York Floods 117
Be Careful 118
Tortoises 119
The Point of Men 120
Full Fruit Salad 120
Dear Rucksack 121
In My Day 122
Donor 122
How to Spot a Poet 123
The Other House 124

THE RUBY SLIPPERS (2011)
Quiet Auditorium 125
On Wearing My Uncle Patrick's
    Hat 126
The Grenz 127
The Dancing Room 128
My Red Sandals 130
Racing Caterpillars 132
The Gift 133
Bless This Handbag 134
Avoiding Stories 136
Sandra is a Child of Peace and
    Love 138

Why I Fancy Him   140
The Ruby Slippers   141
The Green Field   143
Owls   144
At the Foreigners' Club   145
On the 14th Deck of the Cruise Ship Aurora   146
The Rehabilitation Hobbies Room   147
Stay in Touch   148
Drawing Dogs   149
The Shape of Hands   150
Tomorrow   151
The Road Out of Town   152

AND GOD SAID LET THERE BE CHOCOLATE (2013)

And God Said Let There Be Chocolate   153
Chocolate Credo   154
The Refuseniks   155
The Little Chocolate Soldier   156
In Which Dad is 'Dances With Chocolate'   157
The Creature from the Chocolate Lagoon   158
The Smarties Room   159
The Chocolate Angel   160
Dad and Terry's Factory   161
Uncle Pa's Drawer   162
The Empress of Chocolate   162
Les Petits Chiens de Paris   163
The Chocolate Bird in the Garden   164

HERE'S LOOKING AT YOU, KID (2014)

Here's Looking at You, Kid   165
Dad's Lingo   166
The Kids with the Tree House   167
Hospital Lingo   167
French Cat in French Window   169
The Serving Girl   170
The Old Pig   172
The Kindness Medal   173
My Wild Mother   174
The Christmas Letter   176
Eight o'clock in Britain   178
All you need is love   180
Sixties Anthem   182
Baxter's Crime   183
The Kindness of Dogs   184
Distance   185
A wheelchair goes into a bar   185
The Open Door   187
The Lucky Dip Machine of the Magic Bird of Fortune   188
My Mother, the Mustang   189
What They Found in the Poet's Stomach   190
Keats in Piazza Navona   191
Watcher of the Skies   192
The Romany Ghosts of My Father   193
The Green Piano   195
Starting Over   196

AMERICANA (2015)
The letter that never came for the old song and dance man 197
Route 66 198
The Cakes at Walts 198
The Basement Kids 200
Fireflies in Melanie's Garden 201
Racoon Runs for President 202
Bob Goes for Popcorn 203
The Chicago Drug Guy 204
That Lady Liberty 204
The Cuban Lady 205
So, what's the deal New York? 205
Empire State Violation 206
In Which I Dream of Rats 207
Pushing 208
The John Lennon Doorman 209
A Few Dollars More 210
Heatwave, Rhode Island 210
Joleen, Joleen 211
The Man on Wickenden Street 212
Emily's Dress 212
In Emily Dickinson's Garden 214
Americano Pizza 215
Better Late Than Never 216

FROM THE ORIGAMI POEMS PROJECT (2010-2016)
The Whisper of Birds 217
The Russian Doll that Was My Mother 218
Walking the Dog 218
Beer 219
The Midnight Boat 219
The Moon Crying 220
Bonsai 220
The Blind Dog 221
The Littlest Hobo 222
The Leaves of Dachau 223
The Last Time 224
Two Dreams 224
Visiting the Parrot 225
What I Meant to Do 226
All I Want 226
Moments 227
The Healing Pool 228
Different Snowdrops 228
Indigo 229
Inside a Dog's Head 230
Dances With Dogs 231
The Sulking Dog 232
Man Sweeping Leaves 232
Once I Knew 233
Snowed In 234
The Poolside Babes 234
The Dogs of Corfu 235
Under the Old Tree, Corfu Town 236
A Certain Kind of Mist 237
Picasso Woman 238
Glass Robins 238
Ballad of Penny Lane 239
Ringo's House 240
The Trees at the Cemetery 242
Flowers by the Roadside 243
Climbing Trees 244
If I had never seen a butterfly 246
The Valley of Happy Songs 246
New Childhood 247
Leaving Messages in Trees 248

Sculpture by Pete Mayer

View from Helen's back door

Author's Introduction

Sometimes, a poem begins like a song. Sometimes, a poem begins like a melody in the mind, or falls to earth from the moon, or shines in your eyes like the sun. Sometimes a poem is a story you have always known needed telling, or perhaps it is a soundscape of many different stories. Which the next one will be, I am never entirely sure; that is the joy and the fun and the challenge of writing.

The first poems in this book were written in 1969, in my parents' garden, filtered through the sunlight of the old lilac and laburnum trees we had back then. These were my first captive thoughts, as it were, and perhaps now they are gathering their freedom back? I like to think so. Even words have a right to be free and wander the world as they would wish.

Over those weeks I filled three notebooks with brief poems, not really knowing what a poem was. I was inspired by a Dylan Thomas book a friend had brought round. I read 'Fern Hill' as if those were the first words I had ever read. I remember thinking: *if I could achieve a tiny part of anything like that*… and a shiver of wonderment went through me. And I suppose I have been writing to that end ever since.

The poems that follow come from the many different chapters of my life, enriched (I hope) by my travels to Greece, Paris, Venice, Belgium, America and to so many other places. I never set out to write a specific poem, but rather the poem chooses me. It dazzles me, it upends me, it freefalls from the sky, it filters through the branches of lilac, it plays noughts and crosses with me, it sings and dances with me. And I have no choice but to write the poem and honour its voice. I'll be honest; I love words. Luckily Phil, my partner, loves the same words!

I don't know for certain what poetry means to me, and I hope it stays that way. I prefer the voice that comes from the unknown. I like to think of these poems as small wild sparrows that are finding their voice through me. They have travelled through time and space with me; some are thoughtful, some are cheeky. Some, I hope, will make you laugh, while others may make you cry. Maybe both?

Poetry is a way of reaching out to people, and if I can continue to do that, writing that first poem will, I reckon, have been worth it.

Helen Burke
April 2017

Editor's Introduction

I love this book. Which is just as well since, to date, I've spent twenty months working on it – at varying degrees of concentration – and it still hasn't made it to the printers! It's been a long gestation, but not a painful one; you'll see why this is an apt metaphor shortly.

By February 2016, I had already spent months getting my head around Helen's vast back-catalogue; I had a half-dozen Helen Burke pamphlets open on my desk the day me and Mrs McGarry found out we were going to be parents. (Perhaps they work like a fertility charm? Best not investigate that.) My expanding wife then spent much of the summer typing up poems from Helen's older publications, doing an impeccable job, while I headed to York to gather even more material, straight from the source.

As the first officially-scheduled release date came and went, we were in hospital bringing our son into the world. When the second whooshed past in February 2017, we were juggling a five-month-old. By the time you're actually reading this, George will probably be considering which GCSEs to take – but if the finished book is half as magnificent as I expect, it will have been worth the wait.

In a sense, I've only got myself to blame. Helen had been writing poems, and collecting them in various pamphlets, for several decades by the time I met her as a fresh-faced aspiring publisher in 2009. When I embarked on running Valley Press as a business, in early 2011, I wrote to Helen and asked if she'd like to work on a 'proper book', which became *The Ruby Slippers*; a few years later, we collaborated again on *Here's Looking at You Kid*. These were both 'slim volumes', cherry-picking popular poems from across Helen's career, and a third such book was on the cards for 2016.

That's when I got a little ambitious. This time, I didn't want to make *a few more* of Helen's poems available to the public; I wanted to collect and publish *all of them*. That is, everything that had appeared between the covers of a printed book since Helen first put pen to paper in 1969 – and we threw in a few of Helen's very first, hitherto-unpublished poems written in '69 itself, too. (There are hundreds more poems in existence that never made it into any book, and new verses being written every day; but I'll have to tackle those another time. You've got enough to be going on with here!)

I went about this epic undertaking as follows: first, I collected all the original publications (some of which I owned, others were down to a single copy in Helen's attic), then figured out which poems appeared where, which version was the most recent, and assembled them all into a single document. For this, Helen let me take home all the text files relating to poetry on her computer – there were 4,557, if anyone's wondering – and I relied on Mrs McGarry's typing skills for anything pre-dating the poet 'going digital' in 2001.

With the file assembled, I meticulously went through the resulting 46,000 words of poetry, making sure no errors had crept in, and that the style of grammar was consistent – so that even when the grammar went completely wacky, with a ten-dash four-bracket sentence, it was at least *consistently* wacky. I then had a couple of other proofers check the results; this stage easily took 100 hours. (I mention this not to boast or complain, but to give you an idea of what goes into a project of this magnitude – and why you have to hand over such a chunky sum of money to own the final book!) Despite our efforts, there are bound to be a few tiny errors remaining; if you spot one, please let us know for reprints and the ebook edition.

That brings things up to date: now, just a week of light design work stands between these poems and the print factory – a process which obviously went without a hitch, as you're currently reading this on paper between some charming red covers. I must mention here the efforts of fellow Valley Press poet Jo Brandon; I put Jo in charge of ordering and editing the 'notes' section which comes after the poems, which was a whole separate undertaking in itself. It's a tradition for Helen's books to end with some brief notes on the poems, so we hope you appreciate having them here too.

At the back, we've also provided a list of all the poems in alphabetical order, by title *and* by first line, to help you find the one you're looking for in cases of emergency (don't scoff; this will definitely happen). As you'll see, the main text is in chronological order, arranged under the titles of Helen's various books and pamphlets; their years of publication being the only reliable dates we've got. Each poem appears under the title of the book it *first* appeared in, but where multiple versions of poems were published over the years, we used the most recent version – does that make sense? So although 'Tigers' first appeared in the 1995 pamphlet titled *Poetry*, and opens that section in this volume, the version used is from *The Ruby Slippers* in 2011 (and actually, was tweaked again for this book).

The final section of poems didn't appear in a single book; they appeared in a dozen tiny, foldable pamphlets between 2010 and 2016 from the wonderful Origami Poems Project, who have been one of Helen's most prolific publishers over the years. Huge thanks are due to Jan Keough, who provided me with the edited texts for all these; what a star. I must also thank my 'Assistant Publisher' Jo Haywood for her contributions in the final weeks, and Helen's partner Phil, a tireless supporter of the project. Oh, and Helen herself for being so patient, and trusting me to do justice to her life's work – it's been a real privilege. (I'd best thank Mrs McGarry again here too, if I want any tea tonight.)

One question remains: why did I go to such lengths in the first place? Read on, and you'll have the answer; these poems are so utterly unique – or as Paula Meehan wrote, 'of the planet Burke' – that for them to not be readily available to the book-buying public seemed like a crime against literature. When Helen puts pen to paper (or fingers to keyboard) it's more than art, skill and craft; there's a real magic at work. Every word comes straight from the heart of an extraordinary woman, whose whole life is here, compressed into 300 pages – I hope you enjoy reading them as much as I will, in the years to come. (Though I may skip over this bit.)

Jamie McGarry
April 2017

for Phil, my heart, my soul, and my always

and the best Mam and Dad in the world

— from the garden (1969) —

Love is the Feeling Between Now and Now

Love is not the old lady at home all alone,
love is a kiss when the astronauts touch down
oh quick oh you're not looking...

Love is feeling important enough to write in your diary.
Love is the meaning of that sign, 'just gone home'.
Love is saying goodbye and smiling.
Love is saying hello and crying.
Love is putting the fire brigade out.

Love is breaking 'Je t'aime' on his head in a fight.
Love is 12½ stone – not fat but just right.
Love is eating caviar with your spoon.
Love isn't a flat, it's a well-furnished room.

Love is John and Mary, Peter and Janet, Nigel and Rodney –
Tom, Dick *and* Alice –

Love is your umbrella on the wet Monday morning.
Love is laughing at people trying to write poems
trying to explain what
love is...

The Skyline

The day you notice
the blue –
        the sky (where I stand)
I will remove my hat and reveal
3000 bluebirds with carnations tight in their mouths.

The Lens of the Camera

must have been wrong;
my heart is in my eyes
and my sadness is all gone.

— from *A Game of Two Halves* (1979) —

Welcome

In other languages
there are words for it.
'A welcome given is a welcome found,'
but we have none, no such tall or tender
carriages to ride in, no careful gifts
to unwrap, gladly.
How many words for peace lie
stale, unused, fallow?
One field of them? Two fields?
While we labour at some other plough
turn up black turf, until there seems
no end of it.

Piano

Autumn is falling outside,
the room has become dark with the leaves.
They mask the stars in the window.
The room appears smaller, and the flat shape
of the piano, there, against the wall
is my other limb in the darkness.
The night is the shape of hands.
The wood of the piano is the night itself but
no one is here to play it.
No one sees it, the shape of the leaves,
each one a note, continue to fall.
The room collects them.
Can no one see? Can no one hear?
Can no one play the night?

Heart

I have walked round them all today,
all the turrets, battlements and landing points
of your heart.
If you were to walk in now, I could draw it for you
and I do not draw well.
The winding stairs, the minstrelled
upper gallery I have seen, and that most
secret of doors where smooth passages slide
taking us in to the inner chamber,
where no shadows lengthen.
You are in that place now I think.

It is a master craftsman who has built here.
On my walk I saw no unfinished or badly-made
rough markings, no poor materials.
Only quality marked out my route and for
some of the way I cried to see such
familiar friends – such well known words,
remembered sights.
I half expected you around each next and every corner.

But, the heart has a mind of its own.
It does not always weigh up or guess the future
and cannot live upon what's gone and passed.
It simply beats. It is a stickler for beating.
In fact, it insists on it.
If you were to walk in now, I would beat it for you
until the gates above and below us rang out to the sound.
Until the sound itself was felt more so than heard.
In fact I would insist on it, and
I do not beat well.

Poem for Mrs Waters

She drowned kittens. Laid people out.
All the special tasks.
The skills handed on from her mother who
laid them out, before her.

Something about pennies on the eyes,
and a stone in the mouth – or
maybe, the other way around.
Anyway, to simplify the journey

being the general idea.
Her garden was full of flowers grown
for their height. That's right – she did
the flowers as well as a
sort of sideline. But

the main piece of it was the
comfort it provided – just the fact she was
there, could be called, when needed.
Always discreet and
never came to the 'do' afterwards, at the house.

Once she gave me some rosary-beads
the size of apple pips, they hung on milk-thin
silver thread.
They seemed to me to hang like loosened
silver teeth.
She hid them inside an Easter egg; the
two halves split open, laughed at me
like wolves' lips.

She had no children
and used to spoil me. No one took
notes from her, or learnt her trade.
All I remember now is that,
after she died, they gave the pennies away.

Batsi, Andros

People walking by the water's edge are
drawn to the dappled moon
on the white boats.
Their faces are white diamonds
in the night.
They are telling their secrets
to the boats.

The boats whisper then back into
the road of sky, the paths
amethyst, above your head.

The secrets sway with the tide, in and out.
The boats nudge together.
Just shapes in the dark – they whisper,
'You can trust us with that one,
tell us more, tell us more,
who could we tell? – We're just
one little ocean, a few stars,
half-a-moon…'

Foreigner

Standing outside the glass phone booth
I look across at your reflection.
Your feet are perfect, wounded
broad and golden in simple
leather sandals.
I look down at mine –
they are all long bone and odd question marks.
You cross the hot of the street and without
looking directly at me, say –
'Could you make it back home, back to England
without me, I mean?'
I look down at the ground that swallows me and say,
'Of course I could, I've got feet haven't I.'
My smile is stretched, real thin, papier-mache, tired
but, you don't notice this.
'I have to go now,' you say.
As I fall asleep I can hear
the sound of white waves falling
into the black night.
I dream of your thumbprints clear on the new glass.
I try to call home but my voice
is a foreigner. It comes from a long way away
where the sea has no deeper echoes and the
bones of buried sailors shine like ice.

In May

Be careful of May.
It does not sit squarely.
When you see the lilac spires
begin to climb
so much taller than last year,
when the church bell sounds
a little louder than then –
come sit with me.

Come sit with me
when the fragrant moon spills
over our heads onto this would-be
page, colours of half-way into
bloom, where it stands
like an old gardener casting seeds
like runes from under his torchlit
black-cat cape.

I am still mortal in my planting
in what is left to us of May.
Your generous touch on my mute
lines is gone.
You are still my only safe leaning,
although from somewhere else you are
holding me now.
I hear your voice whisper to me,
still, 'take care – you should take care in May.'

The calling song of the bright-eyed
blackbird over our door is here.
How often have we stood
and watched its flight?
I borrow its sweet notes now, and
watch its flight through the
pieces of sky sketched in between
the lilac leaves.

Come sit with me, sit with me,
in what is left to us of May
where forget-me-nots lie down
their heads, where memories root,
and May, so full of spirit
must begin to warmth again.

Lacing Boots

They were narrow, beautiful.
We laced them with finesse.
At lunch hours, pretended we were skaters.
Foreign – mystical enchantresses.

We ran them through the long garden,
down the cinder track, then, through
the wildest stretch, to the tennis courts
and back again.

Folding them, the soft skin doubled over.
Back into our secret locker. In bold
brown brogues we re-appeared
at Latin, double French and Scripture – just as we were
to all around, our feet and hair, neat,
fastened firmly down.
Only ourselves aware that outside two gazelles
were running still,
through the long grass towards
the tennis courts – and on.

The Film

We queued to be a part of it.
The film.
Made originally in India, now Smethwick.
We put saris on over our jeans and, coughing,
smoked exotic black cheroots.

Some of us tried to look tall. Others of us tried
to look 'undiscovered', in a discovered sort of way.
My friend Angela tried to look devil-may-care but with
a deeper poetic side to her, if asked.
I tried to look like a painting, a gouache,
something in miniature. No, definitely not an oil.
Too tacky.

Rumours spread like wildfire down the corridor
as to the real requirements.
Only a bearded man, his odourless feet
on a desk in a side room, we were told, was privy.
The word was he had three navels and two heads.
Just another tea-boy made good, we supposed.
Anyway.

He was the Big One. The main man. Mr Hot and Shot.
If he didn't look at you, you were in with a chance.
If he didn't look at you twice – you were as good as made.
Laughing all the way to the Smethwick NatWest.
Everyone avoided looking at everyone else and several
people mistakenly formed relationships with
water dispensers and fire hydrants.
The corridor grew in length and coffee cups and paranoia.

People dyed their hair. Some, in desperation, back to its
original colour. Some of the women
grew beards. Some of the beards got starring parts.
It was hard to say what to grow or what to shave for the best.

Some of the people around me thought
it all might hinge on faith, so they invented a new religion.
By lunch-time there had been a schism, two rebellions
and a new wave backlash.
In a small side room the navels took turns to be contemplated.

Two people made a film of the corridor – *The Hell That Was
   Smethwick* – and
won an award. No one dared leave to eat.
The only food left was a tube of Smarties.
These were auctioned off by the New Wave Buddhists
Against Beards sect. Some of the Smarties were fakes.
Some people happily ate shirt buttons and said
they liked the orange ones best.
For two Smarties you got to sleep with the Director.
For three Smarties he stayed awake.
Some people tried to smoke them and one man made a cake out of
the cardboard tube.
You could tell the people who had been Smartied –
the pupils of their eyes were orange.

In a last desperate bid, my friend and I tried to look
alone, but as though we were in a crowd, but yet
wanting to be more alone, in a strangely, and wistfully,
almost achingly-approachable sort of way. And yet.
Alone.
Nothing happened, so the rest of us
went home, tried to unpick saris and sequins from our jeans
and looked to see what was on TV that
wasn't set in bloody India or bloody Smethwick.

The Aunts

They sit about my house, the aunts –
drink tea, play cards and laugh.
They sit about my house.
I listen to them.

Sarah, tall and wiry, strong of arm,
and Lella, more delicate, lying
on the sofa, to catch again
her breath.

They sit about my house. I hear the aunts,
their easy talk and laughter,
their tales of people long since gone,
their talk of you.
I hear them best when I remember you.

The sound of their words, soft
doves upon the air –
burrs caught up in downy cloth,
their talk of better days
and times to come.

Sitting, watching the coals glow
in my fireplace – as though
the aunts still breathed on them, they glow.
I breathe in and out with them,
willing them to go on – but even the tallest
of the flames dies away and the last
of the warm embers I see is
also stopped for breath.

Windmills

Cilla dances, and there
is much of chaos in it,
but also much of stillness.
(My chaos goes with a difference.)
Cilla bends to chaos, and chaos
bends with her.
It is a kind of exercise –
sometimes she is a tango, sometimes a waltz,
a stream of atoms, dancing.
'I am learning, but too fast,' I say –
'We must be our own lessons, our own
teacher and go step-by-giddy-step,' she says.

In the class we learn how to be trees,
then flowers, then – 'cottages with hats on' –
such fine windmills!
We worry that chaos has no hat,
and the air here so changed, so chill.
Leaving, we tango-waltz across the grass
(we are not allowed to walk here).
We are angels riding on a single swan's back,
we clearly have the ear of the moon and almost
that of the sun. 'Keep off our cottages,' we shout –
'we are two small windmills, we are chaos,
with hats on!'

Sun

I am catching the last of the sun
as it borrows the edge of the world,
as it smoothes its threaded hold on
the tiles at the end of our wall
where the washing line greets next-door's
sunny climbers.

Leaves from last year's nesting birds
fall onto the table. Dropped outside –
you would wonder who has moved it here
for me. *A friend*, I would say; *not too
close a friend*, you would say, and smile.

Other friends sit here with me now,
and we catch the last of the sun.
But the final rays of it fall on me later,
as I sit here with you, alone,
as I hold you and the sun very close,
as we take what is left, what remains of the sun
before you must return,
where all things are balanced,
on the edge of an always-drowning world.

The Prepared Room

Someone's breath has been left here
in the prepared room –
a ring of chairs, like a corn circle they stand
ready and waiting.

Soft and subtle, the blueness of the curtains
is hung, gradually the backdrop lengthens.
The sides of the room are scenery only,
a temporary stage, newly propped.
There are places, corners painted here
that only the prepared room is aware of.

It knows I should not be here, am out of my time.
I am a charlatan, an imposter, unprepared
for what tomorrow may or may not
bring to this place.

The water jug and the six glasses on the desk
are silent, make not one chink.
The blackboard is eerily close-lipped too.
One phrase, in readiness, on it reads –
'Collect your name-badges from the box
by the door, as you leave.'

To be re-christened, like a new beginning,
feels good, a shined-up apple.
The old name: a dusty cage, a timetrap.
In time all the old names will be left here,
invisible, poor jottings.
Piles of them in the box by the door, slowly
fading from soft white to something subtle, blue.
Gradually the backdrop lengthens.

At Highfield

Next to the bird-table,
where the white cat stalks,
we sit, side by side
under the heavy circling of fir trees
and grey-silk clouds, free-falling tumblers.

A crow flies over us – picks off the table's
choicest bits.
A fat pigeon comes now and then
to check what's left –
breast bulging – small head, army-grey.

A small bird, black and white, stands
firm – Joy says, 'It's a wagtail.'
It mouths straight at us: 'What am I –
am I paper? Am I scissors? Am I stone?'
Its small beak holds the long notes.
Other birds fly to and from the table,
their reflections, brief outlines
in the high windows.

Between us and the table
there are strange white grasses, Japanese.
We can reach out our hands to them, just,
and slowly bend them into
graceful arcs and dancing arabesques.

A lady behind me says, 'Let's hide in the trees
when they come for us', but Joy says, 'No,
let's hide in the soft, smooth grasses, very deep –
or under that white cat's paw, like Alice
in her through-the-glass world.' But
today, I don't want to hide, I want to go
where the wagtail goes, be a thing
quite black and white.

I want to dance above the lingering trees;
call out with him, to the sky, *look at me*.
I too can sing, I too can ask, 'What am I?
Am I paper? Am I scissors? Am I stone?'

At Elvington

The route through the churchyard
is difficult and overgrown,
and though I pick my way,
I always lose it.

With what
dreadful stillness, what
terrible certainty, we move towards
'his favourite flowers', 'her favourite hymn'.
People now remembered as small pictures of themselves –
a child sitting on a father's knee,
a bowing of the legs on the long walk home,
a line near the edges of the eyes
that became gradually and finally
more marked in the sun.

— from *Leros: Island of Dreams* (1994) —

Arrival – Leros

Laugh and see
how
the old beast stirs again
and says:
'I am beauty – I will make you feel me,
I will make you touch me.
You will walk again within me, for
I am the forest that shelters, that shades.
In the cool of the evening
let my blue fringe be your cradle,
let the sway of my ribbon in your hair
give you rest.'

Here – Now

Imagine.
There is just this.
The barely-pink house, the central white archway
then beyond in the waves,
an eagle on top of a column balancing.

A stone falls from the roof.
Its breath lands with it.
Tomorrow, another stone will fall.

Horses' hooves die away,
leaving only the sound of the footfalls of ants,
bees, a cricket, my own fattened breathing.
A swallow flies over me.

There is the sound of his wings
and beyond that, the waves.

Wing

The sea is a single blue banana
pouring into an envelope of
complete light.
There are no patches of mist in this sky,
no question of silver in this sea.
How easy it all makes itself here.

Further along the road today, we came
to a small hedge; on it lay
an oyster-grey, smooth, slicked-back
abandoned gull's wing.
The wing that could be my own. In fact,

you laugh and say you are sure it is
and now I look closer – I recognise it
and remember the loss.
I replace it carefully, at my outer and thinnest
edge, under my ragged sword wing, my battle arm.

There is not enough room for it, it seems to me,
but you take it from me and show me where it fits,
(how easy you make it look) saying –
'Come, let us share the wing. For it seems to me,
we are in the same sky.'

Ankle-Deep

Digging ourselves further into the sand,
Michael shows me how to rock my ankle:
'Begin with this and then progress to an all-round roll.'
I do.
A boat with nine small purple lights comes in,
then goes out behind us – no crew
just the lights that tack themselves
briefly through our eyes.
The boat rolls with the waves, we roll in the sand,
treading away and towards each other, carefully.
We walk up and down the sand. Michael says:
'We move all our bones best, when we appear to
stay in one place. Nothing is all of a piece –
least of all the things we put weight on.'

Swallows at Aghia

We are lying just below where the swallows lie,
watching them build their house.
It is a thousand different shapes of blue.
It takes on their shape.
It is small, low. It is under the sky.
Who may live there, you ask?
Why, a man who has grown old may.
So old, he has become cicada.
He is inside the house;
he winds himself against all of the doors,
hopes for small unlooked-for windows.
He takes on its shape.
The house is small, low. It is under the sky.
He is grateful for it.
Now, we are watching the sparrows
building the sky, a thousand different shades of blue.
It is small, low – under the house –
but it is near, and *so* close to me.
I can touch it with my hand – can't you?
I can wrap my smallest finger right around it.
It unfolds like a fine rose – each petal perfect
and so still.
Placed in its separate space – beak by careful beak
like delicate twigs.
How many shades of blue are there, you ask me?
I do not have words for it.
Only the sparrows know them.
The house? Oh yes, the house, it suits them.

Aghia Marina

The day is a rose, a white rose again and here
the bay is a boat
and the boat is a cat. Again.
They are giving me the means to leave the harbour.
If I choose.
I hang around outside the belt shop.
The heat of the day swims right in
under my hat, contrives a little music.
It is the hymn of the sea.
Passing by I could have missed it.
Sometimes I do miss it, but now I hear it.
The bird that flies into my room hears it.
I call him 'Renate' – 'rebirth',
the day is all roses, and boats and cats.
I am no longer sure which is which.
The boat calls out for food.
We climb aboard, the cat and I, and sail away.
Sleep over
nets that are white roses,
to a tune I thought I had forgotten,
and sail away.

Alinda Bay

A small dog is slipping in and out
of the boats,
the fishing nets, the huge anchors
of men's legs, playing
'I can see you. Can you see me?'
Greece is laying down its coat of morning kindness
over the people of the harbour, of the beach.
Only a sugar girl is crying, red-eyed,
a glass of wine in her hand,
wobbling, unsteady on white high heels.
She too is asking:
'I can see you, can you see me?'
The bay has no answer.
The small dog walks home with her.
He is her only guide. Her only friend.
The sugar girls in every harbour.
Wobbling.

At the Castle

At the top of the long hill, when the dust settles,
we can see the castle is padlocked.
We retrace our steps.
As we walk down, Jean and I
try to walk across the solid blue water.
There is a planet of it. A turquoise acre. Untilled.
It has taken us to its heart, this water.
We can walk on anything we want to.

Further down the hill, we watch a windmill
turning in the wide air.
It fans the clouds.
Snatches of a song play up at us.
The notes are strangely high,
and new to us, unsettling.
Above us the castle door is open now, it is
a black half-moon. The clouds seem nearer too.

Jean smiles, says: 'The gates are being closed.
It was just the castle's way of having a bit
of a joke with us. I can see that now.'
But it is too late for us today. We must walk
back up the hill another time, another way.

V.E. Day

Come May – when roses bloom
we can remember.
Dark red the rose that grows on the balcony.
It shines one day, its face so young; just begins
to see the sun, then too soon is picked,
its strength away.

Dawn

And best of all –
when the morning dawns,
clear and bright
and the stars go quietly two by two,
into the eye, the boat of night
and the heart of dawn that
breaks with mine
so briefly gleaned with yours that
was too soon away.

The Traveller

Listen out for me,
who carves you out bright jewels
in the images of night
who sits at your window
to catch your eye, as you awake.

There is no rock,
nor climbing hollow
that is too far for us to travel,
for tonight we are bound together;
though they say I must away, but

listen out for me, as there,
there I go – the traveller.
I am in your sudden softened footstep,
your ears' distant murmur,
even in your gaze as you
stand in wonder at the door –
keep a fire in your hearth for us
who travelled on at dawn.

Villa

The yellow man and the priest
stand on the steps of the villa.
The blueness of their hats surprises me.
That they have arrived is certain, but…
when were they here before?
Why are they here now?
They pretend to whisper, but do not.

The large handles of their urns
catch at our hearts.
In the sun they baffle us.
We look at their photos, the long beards,
the lean cheeks, the woman
with eyes that hold her prisoner.
'Too much of the sight can be a cross,' she says.
We see hers and witness it is.
'Go back, back along the path,'
she calls. We push ourselves quickly along the path
to where the white chapel ends
and the spectrum of the sea begins.

Saint George's Chapel

We stood beneath the candles,
the three of us, the two of you,
smiling.
Upwards hung the light; I thought so then
and now.
The gold altar, the robes of the statue,
the circled roses, the small face of the icon
made an altar itself, half-hidden by gilt birds
and smaller angels.

When the clouds broke, later that day,
the candles were the only light in the long street,
creating a plain gold distance. We watched each of them
casting a single shadow on the crooked arm of the road;
caught ourselves laughing in the lengthening mirror
of their upturned eyes.

For Bob (in Leros)

Where the wild Oxalis blooms,
my love and I walk by,
where St John's bells
reach up and catch, and echo from the sky.
They steal away, my aches, my pains
these thoughts, this self – unreal…

for where the wild oxalis blooms,
there, my love and I walk still.

At Garbo's

Kathleen runs down to see the ferry;
she is quick, the first one there.
She leaves the hamburgers, and runs.
'I don't trust that ferry – any ferry –
if you shake hands with it, you'd better
count your fingers then,' Dave says. He
follows her slowly, down to the harbour.
John drinks his brandy straight off,
catches them up.
Kathleen says: 'This is the "Theatre" island –
even us, we all have parts to play.
Look at us – we're playing them now.'
John says: 'I had a rose, it was beautiful.
It bloomed just once in May.'
Frank, busy in the kitchen, flips the burgers over,
says: 'You've got to count your blessings,
haven't you? You've got to be happy,
while you can. Who knows, tomorrow,
the meltemics may blow.'
John reads Kath and Frank their horoscope.
'It says here you will be leaving Leros,' he reads.
'I too, am leaving Leros but,
it just doesn't say when.'

Patmos

The day is all moon and roses
and boys and cats and boats.
There is no dividing line.
Saint John is a thousand years old today.
He is a hero.
He has brought the rains – gradually
they wash the old street down,
the peeling yellow from the houses
a holy confetti from the holy man.
A bus driver turns his bus on a bend in the road;
it is the size of a Hail Mary.
Some of us have brought our own Hail Marys with us –
we use them now, keeping our eyes tight shut.
Across at Saint John's cave I swear I can hear him
playing poker, sniffing coke, laughing through his beard
at the sudden rain.

Papa Retsina

He is an uncommon priest – our first sighting.
He sits with the ouzo set, and in between
poses for our cameras.
He hardly seems to priest at all.
He does not remind me of Father Donovan at home.
He does much of it now by fax and worry-bead,
he tells us.
He has a son much taller than him, who can
drink more, but still no one here knows his given
name. He is Papa Retsina
when he is known to one and all.

Leros Cat-Walk

I did not know there were two layers to you, island.
Room by room I shall come at you, though my paws
are long and green, as the sea, as the sea. I will swim
this way and that, until higher I am. The whole length of it.
Then, low and flat-lying, I shall look at you, up at you.
When you are not watching, but I am watching you.
My ears will discover you.
I am a delight. No dwelling is as perfect as mine.
My other home is a pale green web, beyond your moon, an
urchin's laugh, a sailor's love for the marble stair,
the angel star
that guides him home, too soon, too soon.
You cannot reel me in, though you think you may
while you walk up and down your second layer,
but all this is my domain now and I never stray.

Vortex

So many stars tonight
and all the people from Leros
who are apart from her tonight
are dreaming the same dream.

At the centre of Leros, they find an apple –
they eat the apple.
Each of the apple pips is a hunter.
Diana is at the apple's core itself;
the red hunter on her green tree.
She is a dove, a mist that rises with the dawn
and draws them ever in.

She chews on Leros, juggles with its mysteries.
Each of her people, new and old, she knows,
helps form. She lays aside her arrows blue,
her arrows gold, then sees them safe ashore.
All the people from Leros are with her tonight –
'How can they be?' you ask … because
tonight they are dreaming the same dream.

Departure

In their hurry,
they left seven roses in the child's room
when they went,
and the light came through the window,
broke fiercely across the petals
from every side, irregardless.

The roses stood for many days in the sun,
with no water, just the encircling light
to filter their breath through.
It was enough.

Kallinichta

My last night in Leros,
I stand opposite to the wishing well
where a donkey is tethered.
The white roses, those perfect faces,
look across kindly at me.
They are small, perfect, ivory kisses.
The sky is heaven's blue, a haven with them.

Greece is always 'now', it is all 'now' –
though the words, were I to say it
would be swallowed whole by the wishing well.

We stand a little while longer, all of us,
watching the 'now' –
the white cat on her wall,
the donkey at his post, and that bird that circles
over our heads
calling out 'I too am part of the dream. All of this
we give to you. Do not forget us.'

— from *Poetry* (1995) —

Tigers

I know there is a beginning and an end to most things
I know that when you're in the middle of two people, one feels left out
I know that between today and tomorrow this or that will happen
I know that when you say you're not worried that is not really how you feel
I know that to be sure of something, even for one minute, holds no eternal guarantee
I know that landscapes where I've lived are still the same – it's me that changes, isn't constant
I know the sea has no enemies
I know that time will tell
I know that without permission everything is possible
I know religion is no excuse
I know love is a word in need of translation
I know to start caring again is as hard as to stop
I know today has no roof and yesterday has no mirror
I know that life is probably not a film someone has made
I know that there are people who never dream
I know that to dream of white means death
I know that to dream of tigers, always of tigers, is unlikely and not to be wished for, but nonetheless I do –
and I know that tigers should not be held by their tails.

New Girl at the Shop

We were almost engaged,
we had sort of plumped for the beige
when she swanned in;
with her fast-track talk of swish-and-glide.
You were soon blinded by her floor-length verticals –
you were on the horizontal from the first.
Your eyes – a glazed no-turning-backness –
a blackness – all ablaze you were,
with one withering look that said
'all-the-way-from-here-to-soft-furnishings'.
It was as simple as that, you see.

You shared your bar of fruit and nut
with her, on the way home, and
I knew then it was 'curtains' for me.

Map

Give a man a map
and he will study it.
I study the landscape,
you study the map.
We re-read *War and Peace*,
we eat what's left of the pastilles,
you study the map.

It was summer, quite pleasant
when we set off – now, outside, the
waves are beginning to change, and fall,
to cling to the wet road.
We study the markings on the leaves, their
colour, their fragility, the
shortness of life, is there, is there not
a God?

We drive down one road,
we drive up another. We arrive
somewhere, we leave somewhere.
We leave it again.
A man is passing by. You stop him.
You are keen and ask him
to study the map. He
looks at you strangely.

He has just arrived from Gothenburg.
He is here for the swimming.
He is a twin town. Around his eyes
he has laugh-lines.
But he does not laugh. When he goes –
you study the map.

We stop outside a church. The United
Reformed Saint for the DIY-Afflicted.
We get out to stretch our legs.
We discover we have arrived at Cherry Road,
in fact we are opposite number 42
and friends are waving.
But you have no faith in it and do not
see them.
It is the map and you against the world.

We look around for you – to break the news,
but you have returned to the car.
We glimpse you slumped across parts
of Worcestershire.
You are near-exhausted; you look ethereal,
fey, not of this world.
We could forgive you, almost, almost.
But something wild, primeval, drives me
too now.
So we take the last packet of mints
and leave you.
You are sleeping now, but I know you.
Even in your dreams, and across much bigger borders,
don't think I don't know, it's you
studying the map.

Fireworks

You had a special way
of building a fire.
Quick, urgent, armfuls of wood, hunted
twigs and corkscrew-papers hurled,
charmed, into oblivion.
Sweet-talked, it always lit
first-time.

A few mocked, envied
your madcap dance. Logs hammered home
to certain angles, hunks of coal hand-hugged,
your face as black as they –
all grit, no shine and on the chin
a layer of fine coal-dust.

From your pocket hangs,
one corner only visible, a half-black
half-white handkerchief. I can still see it.
The image as bright as the gold flame ladder
climbing high behind your hands, and it too
always, always lights –
first time.

Space

'It's as though something is
constricting me,' he said,
'I need to move around –
feel as if I can, at least – all this junk!'
She sold her mother's old sofa, the two
battered chairs, and that seemed to help
for a while, then –

'I still feel if I had
a larger area to breathe in I wouldn't
be so irritable, tired all the time. What's wrong?
I just told you, I need area – that's what's wrong.'

The cooker and the gas fire went next; it
was a bit cold and the fish and chip diet
brought her out in spots, but
what the hell, you had to work out these things.
She had read about it in *Cosmopolitan*.
It got easier after that.

The record player, the toasters, the cat –
she scarcely missed them. Then, flattened against
the balcony one day, difficult to iron on such
a very narrow ledge, she felt the door closing
slowly outwards, pushing against her chest,
squeezing her breath slowly out, out,
and a breezy voice floated to her, saying:
'At last, I don't know why I didn't think of this before.'

Walkers

Down to the waterfall and back
is not far for them.

The reaches of their feet and arms
are long – they reach the top in FOUR.

Two pairs of arms wave down
across slicing rain and bracken that is black-gold.

They crawl back through the car like
two water-rats getting in a tumble-drier.
We fast spin them around, drive them to the top again,
but the top is now the bottom for them –
(this lady has been sawn in half).
It's boring now, and 'bloody raining' and
'can we find a McDonald's, please – or go home'.

The Op

'It's not so bad,' he calls out.
'What's that?' asks the little deaf man.
'She's only down for the leg, I think,' he calls again.
'Oh, not so bad then,' a high voice that lives
on the ceiling replies.
My story is repeated all the way down the ward
like a sinister, Chinese whisper.
As it finally freefalls into Sister's room,
she checks the name, colours it yellow,
marks it 'X'.
The man in the bottom bed, who started the whisper,
is now telling the nurse a joke – the one about the surgeon
and the duck. The nurse moves gamely on, shouts:
'How is your dog now, then?' to a woman
behind a screen (Greta) – 'having a bad day'.
Did I tell them the piano was to go to Bob? I think, as
I am wheeled at speed past Gloria, who is knitting, and
two old ladies, beaming, having their hair
scalpelled into newness; the fools, all of them.
'We've ordered you the lamb,' they shout. 'But not the apricot.'
I wave my hand at them, and they wave back, from
a fluffed-out, pink-permed distance, like novice Buddhas.
We all wave lots of hands,
at least three per wrist.

Sheep

Sheep are odd.
Sheep are desirous to be told things.
They wait open-mouthed for you to speak to them,
then clank away.
Sheep are always mutton dressed as lamb
and many are forced to join Gambollers Anonymous.
Their favourite games are Snap and Follow my Bleater.
Their favourite film is *War of the Wools*.
They play music by Ab-baa and Hoofenbach
and many prize an autograph by Placido Merino
worn on the left buttock.
Their favourite cocktail is
a sloe-comfortable-spew-against-the-rocks.
Sheep like to party (their red eyes are a giveaway).
Sheep do a lot of grass.
They make lousy rickshaw drivers
preferring to ride tandem in groups of four or fourteen.
Sheep's favourite saying is:
'one swallow does not a mint sauce make.'
No sheep has ever stood for Parliament
but there are many sheep there.
Sheep always wear white at night, for safety,
and are keen to holiday in Baali or Ramsgate.
Sheep's favourite words are barnacle or Baa-nard Castle,
but they dislike the word baa-becue and rarely finish it.

Fever Flowers

They are prepared to dig a little deeper,
to leave my space, also
(Heather tells me this, later, in the car,
on the way to see Shelley.)

Shelley asks – 'Why have we all brought
so many flowers?' But, why have we?
When those people there, inside the earth,
can only see the stalks of the flowers
(no matter how carefully we arrange them,
lay them out exact, inch by viewed inch.)

Her small bones are pale today.
The special fever medicine that sits
in mum's fridge is bottled wizard's blood,
and is *good*. It blots out
the bad hotness from her head.
Over the sink,
we watch a small thrush
move skilfully across the lawn,
we watch it peck around the flowers,
piercing them gently, stalk sides up.

The Flying Suit

I sleep fully-clothed in case
you should need me –
I am on the outside edge of the bed
to make an immediate response to your call.
My pyjamas are tense, so tense
I may have to snap the stripes to break free
when your call comes – to reach your voice
through the buzzing of static air.
The shoes on my feet are running shoes,
the switch for the light is one inch from my hand;
I have measured it.
I want only to milk your words of blood, your
soul of tissue, muscle, down this fatted artery
blocked with nerves.
No, I do not feel this is extreme, at all,
why do you ask?

Beneath my right arm is one phone.
Beneath my left arm is another phone, in case
the first should prove faulty.
I do not take chances with fate.
If I were psychic, I could anticipate your voice,
exhibit a crystal calm, and time my response – but
as I am not, I must check and re-check the cable
that leads to the box that leads to the floor,
that connects my wire to your wire.
Everything is fine, here, in working order;
I keep the phones here in case you should need me,
and I sleep fully-clothed, in a flying suit.

George

George sits on the corner of
our street. He is having his
first meal of the day – a boiled sweet.
It is an unwrapped boiled sweet;
George believes that wrapped
boiled sweets and foreigners
are infiltrating the country
like a slow poison.

He himself is vetting as many
boiled sweets as he can,
but one man can only do so much.
It is a thankless task and still he
sticks to it.
He takes out his pen to deliver
the first letter of the day
to the Queen, to inform her of his progress.
An American is passing by, and just
in case, he puts his pen away,
and waits.

Oz

You wrote to me of storms,
of unimaginable things happening
on coral reefs, and that
you are close to a girl.

I imagine her like the coral itself;
spiky fingertips, galapagos pigtails,
fine strands of her reaching out to me
across various oceans.

Then you wrote, sorry to have been
of any trouble – apologies if
any emotional hijack had… etcetera, etcetera –
but, could I still store the books, the bits
and pieces, pick-up to be arranged at later date.

These facts washed over me, like dull
high waves over wreckage.
I got over it, but sometimes I dream
of that coral girl, of the blackness
of her hair, and how it must have fanned
across your chest, in sleep,
and of her many eyes, like octopi,
fishing for and finding your soul –
holding it up to the dark, keeping it there.

Leaving

No one wants to be the first to go.
It signifies a certain unease, an ennui.
(Disheartened couples grown sad over the cheeseboard
will ask, before they later sleep.)

We ask for people's presence; request, demand it, almost
seek it like a blessing. But leaving, damnable leaving
is never graceful. Even
ballerinas stumble at this tell-tale kick; at going,
tights akimbo, legs and ribbons all askew.
The better clowns are more adept at this movement
in the general direction of the door. Curling
under it, through it and round it, they show us how.
Let us open it, open it and be done, we think.
Let the open door be finally accepted as friend, not foe.

No one can stay forever – why, this would wear us all out,
and would not be right, not the thing at all.
There would be no room for newer faces, fresher troops,
frisky folks and comers-in, as eager to arrive as
our tired bodies are to leave. But

why is it, as we leave, as we close one door,
the urgency of why we had to go eludes us,
is lost to us once more? Until, as we are greeted
again on the other side by our expectant hosts,
all is recalled. Undaunted, they nod and welcome,
bring us in, old familiar faces, newcomers to
unreal, unchanging places – unsure if they are home.

Another Song

Cutting the road
to a solid edge,
first, the boots welling up –
all dust, and the salt lines,
fresh.
The men start singing, the sweat
rolls down their arms –
the elbows become as sore
as a child's rubbed eyes.
My dad's cap is pulled well down,
over tired, dustbin-lidded eyes.
Sometimes he makes me think
of a snowman, all black where the white
should go, and huddled spaces
for the mouth, the eyes.

They come up from the ground,
singing 'The Rose of Tralee' and 'Danny Boy',
climbing out of the earth –
'grave robbers all of us', they joke, and
'it's our funeral'. Shaking their big fists
at the invading dust.
A part of the road goes home with each of them.
Tomorrow it's pay day.
A good rest tonight, then, a woman
bringing tea in mugs and a thin brown envelope.
Numbered.

Soon, it's Monday again,
and the landlord comes.
'Where's the rent?'
'It's all been spent,' we shout,
sending him on his way
with a flea in his black and blue cap.

Me dad's clean new notes
in his soft-lined pocket and us with
another song to learn
before next week.

Aldeburgh

Under an almost moon-landscape at Aldeburgh,
Bob and I pick shells along the beach.
One in the shape of a tiger's tooth we like best.
We move it along for a while, until it is lost,
mixed in with the rest beneath our
shuffling feet.

You need to rest now, and I need to rest.
It is possible to think that we can here,
by the water's edge. We let each other rest.
The shoreline is a little hazy and the mist
of a fen-tiger is descending.

At night, I am our best shell; you open me,
I listen to the sound of you.
You promise to enfold me finally, when
you are able to send word, but for now
I am not expected home. I keep an eye on
the mist that swallows the wave gradually.
What is this new horizon you are walking on?
There are no visible marks of our walking,
and yet we have crossed over something wide,
something not just reached by land alone.
I send you greetings from the old shore
and can smile now as you send yours back.
We take our rest together, by the water's edge.

On Coats

I'm on coats
down at the hall
where Sister Gerard serves the tea.
I'm holding up a big red coat
for a big red-faced lady to look at.
She likes it.
She likes me. She pats us both.
I parcel up the coat.

Behind the silver tea urn,
the shine of it bigger than myself,
I can look across at Sister;
small black gown, huge white head-dress
like a fruit-bat, the
wingspan is enormous.

I'm still on coats.
I'm holding up a check racing jacket
for a small racing man.
He smiles like a whippet. He likes the coat.
He doesn't like me.
He strokes the coat. His eyes are dark as usherettes.
I parcel up the coat.

Someone brings round the rock cakes.
They've saved me one with chocolates on.
Sister smiles, and pours the tea.
I'd rather have a plain cake, I want to say,
I am not a child.
But I have to smile, and say 'Thank you'.
'Thank you,' I say, then
someone tries a beret on me and laughs;
as though I'm not there, but then
they're not on coats. They're
bric-a-brac.

Coats is an accolade, a thing of honour, set apart.
Coats is John Wayne firing on all cylinders.
Coats is Jimmy Stewart saving the angel.
Coats is Clark Gable not giving a damn.
Coats is no maths homework, and snow in summer.

I'm not on coats; I'm on shoes.
I'm in disgrace.
I misplaced the rock cakes. I said bum
in sister's hearing, so
I'm not on coats.
I could have been the 'little flower' of coats,
I tell my mother.
She suffers the news silently,
and pulls my new beret down over my ears. We walk home
the long way, not through the snicket
where you can bounce against the hedges.
We pass a lot of women in new coats
and one man, with eyes as dark as usherettes,
in a shiny new coat, the pockets bulging,
full of rock-cakes.

Whale

We discussed
when and where whales sleep
(if they even do). How heavy
is a whale's dream? Maybe it can
only dream once a century. All the rest
of its wide-lipped, big-jawed,
muscle-turned, blink-free day – it fits in,
before tackling its first wink,
its first breath, and its last.
Who could stop a whale doing that?

Its swimming is a graceful egg, a perfect
bowl of white lilies, the pure sound
of a Ming vase.
It does not swim, but pipes the ocean
through its veins, once a day –
turns it in one almighty somersault,
straight up, straight over.
The globe, an aristocrat of acrobats,
is a safe tennis ball in its mouth,
spinning effortlessly – taking
its first breath in with its last,
one long slow breath
before the whale can dream again,
before the Earth should chance to cool –
to spin, to stop.

— from *Midnight in the Morning* (1998) —

Hope Street

The people of my father's days
were born on Hope Street.
The street itself, I pass every day.
Sometimes I see their faces in his.

It is a long street now,
and unlined by trees.
Trees would drive a hard bargain
to be welcome here.

Hope Street, as I walk down you
it is as if I am in limbo
between your days and mine.
You never let me cut the corner,
you never let me turn quite back.

Its silent face bears the marks
of all those Irish songs, all those
Irish, magical, music-hall lives turning
on an old barrel-organ.
They all stand recorded here.
Why, I ask, was even one dream
one too many here?

Therapy

Star-gazer Towers, Barnsley East, Monday.
Apparently there will be three stages to my rescue.
On the first day, I will be dressed in blue,
given the name of an Indian river God,
and thrown down a set of mud stairs.
Already, my psyche feels cleansed.

On the second day
a man will explain tantric sex to me
while we await a vegan banquet,
in a tepee he has made himself from drawings
he received, whilst in trance, in a waiting room
at Barnsley railway station.
He also has an Indian name.
He tells me he is Smoking Moon;
that he and his partner, Maureen, or
Grey Owl Who Shops, are twin energies.
He says his days with Relate are 'over' –
behind him now. And I believe him.
All of my chakras are flexing now, and yes, yes,
I'm easier in myself, I proclaim.
Secretly I put it down to tantric sex.

Wednesday.
This afternoon, as I write they will
bear me in a golden chair, across a pit of glowing coals
and anoint me with angelic essences
channelled to the earth via a woman from Merthyr Tydfil
who has had a vision of the earth vibrating
to a new frequency, hers.

Thursday.
Apparently, if I centre my chaos, I still have a chance.
I can still let go, and become
an altogether enlightened and better being.
But, if I let go, I ask,
aren't I simply holding on to letting go?
Wouldn't it be better to let go when my own back was turned
thus taking my karma by surprise as it were?
Grey Owl thinks not.
She feels both my inner child and my higher self
have merged, which in the last analysis, is crap.

Friday.
Tomorrow, everyone leaves for Merthyr Tydfil,
or the new dimension of all parallel truths in the known universe
as it is known to Smoking Moon.
Secretly, I leave a note of apology
in my feng-shui-perma-culture-short-back-and-sides dome,
and take a cab down to the station.
There, I'm sure I'll stay in touch,
at least with myself, and
as I break out the Mars bars, board the train for Doncaster,
it's true I do feel like a new person, only much older.
But, all in all, I think I've had my money's worth.

Mellow Yellow

He is a Peter Pan of the disco scene.
He wears what he wore in the sixties.
He says what he said in the sixties.
He is looking for someone to love him
when he is sixty-four.

He has ten years to go, he has two thousand five
hundred gin slings at the bar left to drink;
whichever way you look at it really.
If you stand him in front of a radio, it automatically
plays a little something by Donovan, wherever in
the world you happen to be.

He never made it to India; he got as far
as Barnsley, then ran out of cigarettes.
Sometimes he sleeps rough in a tepee on his allotment.
He has a spirit guide called Beryl, who has a thing
about phone bills and World War 1. She is a big help.

He has a tuft of grass from Stonehenge and will be
buried with this and a drumstick that belonged to Moonchild,
his ex-wife, who was a close friend of the Applejacks. They
met on Crewe Station. It was a kind of happening. He
was eating a banana, she wasn't.
He is cool, he is hip, he is spaced out
at regular, twenty-year intervals. Catch his act now
while he still has his own caftan, his own teeth.

Foxglove

Foxgloves are a wild flower.
I sleep on a bed of them.
I eat foxglove, dream foxglove.
I am foxglove.

Smooth, purple pockets of foxglove
fill up my eyes. New blood
grows from my nails, washes itself
into my hair.
Foxglove, foxglove.
The colour is insistent. It is
my new colour.
With the colour I am becoming strong. Tall.
It is the colour I am fit for.

The foxglove is neither
fox nor glove but keeps itself, in all,
under wraps, part by painted part.
The colour is as I would wish,
I do not fear them.

I keep some foxgloves in my secret cupboard.
They are as innocent as snow, sweet purple snow,
they can put a spell on you.
But do not fear them, they show you a simple face.

Beyond their face, they cup a wildness
to themselves.
Some turn their faces to the bold sky
and from it take new heart.
Upon you, upon them I shall cast a spell of welcome.
I live. I breathe. I can deny them nothing.
I am foxglove.

Snake

The snake has surrounded itself, it is beside itself
at the water's edge.
It is bigger than its owner.
Its head is a hand in retreat.
It lolls against the smooth bowl of the beggar.
Someone spits in the bowl, misses, hits the snake.
The snake's black-list, in its dark heart, grows.
In the heat, he leaves one skin, enters another.
The snake is beyond reproach for this.
Think, if you could leave your body,
step, like him, into another one,
how much calmer you might feel, or how
much bolder. How much younger, and yet,
so old.
Touching the past with the tip of your tail
and circling your future with the length
of your tongue.

India

This dog, India, has many faces, many masters.
One is like that of a skull on the beach,
another that of a thin dog, an angry dog,
with eyes as grey as sharks' fins;
pinholes, picking out the light.

Yet another is that of the fakir, dripping blood
into small bottles of gold and turquoise.
'I am growing here many things that
may interest you,' the fakir says. 'In one bottle,
I am growing courtesy towards my wife;
in another, a patient ear that I can lend to my brother.
In the last bottle is truth. That one is for herself.'

More faces. This is that of the beggar, hanging
his dhoti out on a line with his teeth.
Then Pinto the taxi driver, whose mother draws
henna snakes on the thin arms of junkies.
The man who sells the coconuts says he has
a poor sister, and she herself a poorer one.
He says her eyes are like midnight in the morning;
they are like the tears of Krishna himself, falling,
falling. In her own room, she has a picture
of Lord Krishna, dancing.

Against the path of withered coconut leaves
these faces fall, one by one.
We throw them up in the air, catch them;
their husks are of the earth, but the crescent moons
of white flesh we bite into so eagerly
only adopt our hunger. They take one hunger from us,
only to give us another.

The City

It is a pageant of owls.
It is a heartbeat sounding clear across the valley.
It is an un-numbered wish.
It is a voyage of endings.
It is a tryst of lovers
on white bridges under a red gypsies' moon;
my friend, this is the city of lanterns.

What do you know of the city of lanterns? Nothing?
Let me tell you.
It already belongs to you.
Its thoughts are like blades of grass,
straight-sprung, many.
It surpasses even a field of daisies,
open-eyed into a world of peace.
The lights that shine there come
not from the city, but from yourself.
There, to wear a ring
drawn from a dead man's finger
is to draw on the nerve that draws
straight from the heart.
You can go there now.
Or, you can go a little later.
But go. YOU ARE EXPECTED.

To find the city,
travel with yourself and be happy to do so.
It is a city not of chance, but of destiny.
No fading realm, but one with thunder at its belly,
and lightning in the bone within.
It has no reason to exist, and so exists.

Let me go there now, you say,
but there is no hurry.
The eye of the city is never far from your wandering.
The city will find you.
It will find you at your coolest and yet brightest hour.
It will shine away all your shadows,
welcome you with joy
when you choose to return.

Sea-Largo

Tonight, I am the sea,
cool and calm,
breaking light into sound
and birds into shadow-lanterns.

Tonight, I am the sea.
I am the music of flutes
beguiling the white-lipped spray.
I am this limbo, wild music for you.
Do you hear me calling, calling
against the rocks?

Tonight, I am the sea.
I am the wild and winding wind that
lives deep there.
I am all the creatures that live by the sea alone.

See where I make my bed in the snakes of sand?
See where the foam coils my hair, where my eyes
lap at the edge of shells?
I make the sound the sea makes at night.
Beneath the waves I reach for the pulse of stars;
the echo of their song is silence.
Tonight, I am the sea.

Irish Funeral

This is no speedy seeing off,
no quick farewell, no fast last words,
and a hell of a hooley at the end of the day
I'll be bound, says me dad.

This encounter with death is done
with luxurious leisure.
There are old ladies in raincoats
like twinkling shells, crinkled shades of peach and pink,
and old retainers in dusted-down army suits,
coracles of hearing-aids slung over freckled ears.

The blonde baby in the front row –
old George's grandson – leads the congregation in crying.
Strangers to the service
huddle behind upside-down hymn books,
their heathen, almost *brazen* breath, betraying them.
The lacquered tusks
of old men's hair shine brightly in this distilled
but still eternal light.

The hooley is four doors further down
and wheelchairs are needed.

Everyone looks at everyone else's faces, keenly as stoats.
All the old men rummage in pockets
for scraps of paper, a number, a name,
something they can hold up to be recognised –
please God let them be recognised.
The leading wheelchair rolls,
orders are placed for the bar –
make mine a double, Dad says, and the talk
goes on.

Gargunnock

An echo has reached me
from your wood.
It says: 'come dance with me.'
It is autumn in your wood. In mine also.
I let the echo reach me through this
long song that is our autumn.
An echo here meets an echo there.
None of this is commonplace.
There is music within the rocks in your wood.
The sky is fastened to the trees' notes in mine.
How is it that within the granite you have caused my sun to rise?
I can hear the birds now, how beautifully they move
in your wood. How they tread my heart back to life
through these pastures of silence. Spring will break through,
light my way again.

The illusion of one tree especially moves me.
It is a red tree, it is dancing.
It keens to remain red. I think it will do so.
In the darkness of the other trees I hold to this one tree,
which is red, which is dancing.
We are kin like the seasons. We are chameleons.
Together we slip back into the ground.
Together we will drink the sky of dreams.
After this one tree comes many other trees, and all of them
are dancing.
Though greenest are the hills that are farthest from me,
and walking home through our wood I do not reach you,
still I greet your echo where it hails me
beyond the finest tree, in the quiet twisting leaves.
Greenest.

Boatman

Against the hut that the boatman keeps
a dog is snivelling and snivelling.
I never saw such a mist before.
I never saw such a dog before.
But where is the boatman who must surely keep this dog?
The boat lies between two sets of blossoms
but of him there is no sign.
This is just my luck, for I have a string of questions
for this skilful fellow
and they will not be quietened.
The oars from his small boat
I can see moving under the bridge, but still
I am not close enough to see the long arms, pushing them.

The significance of today is lost on him.
Boatman, I want to shout,
this is my fullest, final day, my last inshore.
But my voice grows faint, and he, he lies low in his boat.
I must become a reed, nipped by rocks to see him.
I must become a plant that cartwheels in the river's mud.
I must become the scent of orange-blossom that trails
in the current that runs on the far side.
Always I must become one with that current.
The scent of the blossoms will be mine, when the boatman comes.

An old lady at the end of the bridge
is calling her wild geese away from the edge
and back to her.
I let my fingers drowse in the water
that takes the blossoms upstream. Myself, I
am bound for the far side. Slowly, I board.

— from *The Book of Beyond* (2001) —

Recipe for a Poet

First, take an unusual childhood.
By the age of three, you should at least be sporting a wooden leg.
By the age of four, you should be dressed completely in wigs,
pseudo-chess pieces and old sailors' clothes,
preferably without the old sailor being attached.
An eye-glass would also be good.

Your mother should be, unwittingly, a great beauty,
able to paint upside-down in the nude, and take in lodgers
who were once either aristocrats or murderers.
Both would be ideal.
Your father, the seemingly saner one,
should be a Russian Prince, with a liking for cheroots,
balalaikas, and looking mystically out of windows clutching a book.
The book must never be identified. This is crucial.

Don't panic. You're halfway there already.

Next, you should have a half-mad sister, who
makes love to passing tradesmen on the dining room table –
well, any table really –
wearing only wellington boots and fishnet tights.
She is called Esmeralda, but only answers to Gert.
Your older brother, well, let's face it, he can be anything
from an accountant to a taxidermist to a line dancer
(though this last is pushing it).
Older brothers are often irrelevant and he will almost certainly
    outlive you,
so you are allowed to dislike him. Heartily.

Now, we come to you.
You must die young, and be mad, bad and brilliant.
You should practise some incredibly deep last words, like:
'Je ne regrette rien', 'Et tu, Brutus' or
'Okay, I'll see the doctor now.'
You may have 486 lovers – all of whom will speak well of you,
despite the fact that you treat them like lemmings.
In fact, lemmings have it easy, compared to them.

In your teens, if you make it that far,
you should have a completely committed breakdown.
And I don't mean one of those half-hearted affairs,
involving therapy and pleasant chit-chat with other loonies,
sorry, doctors. No. No.
No. I mean really throw yourself in at the deep end.
Pamper yourself. Show the others how it's done.
You must go completely and superbly bonkers.
Here are a few tips, if you're stuck.

Grow an extra nipple.
Change your hairstyle to resemble an anteater's.
Wear a cat as an accessory.
Give one of your eyebrows a separate mailing address.
Call yourself by the name of an undiscovered galaxy.
Take to riding a horse in full armour –
even if it's only to pop down to the local Co-op
for a loaf of bread and a couple of muesli yoghurts.
It's this sort of attention to detail that people notice.
This is what makes the difference between the fourteen-liner
and the card-carrying sonnet scribbler.

Now we come to death.
You should be travelling somewhere distant
(this could even be out-of-body if you're short of cash).
Either you receive a sudden snake or anteater bite
(blame it on the hairstyle) –

or your plane's wind-mobile should fuzz, fur or clog
causing you to make a sudden, unprecipitated, unexpected
and painful crash-landing. Peru is quite popular.
Or Basingstoke. Although obviously pack more sensibly
for Basingstoke.
At any rate, the tribe where you pull up were not anticipating
   visitors,
and catching them rather on the hop, as you do
(and in the absence of their own Co-op)
they invite you to stay for dinner.
Unfortunately for you, young poet, you *are* dinner.

And this is how poets are made.

The Happening

Nothing ever happens.
The postman's wife does not have cancer.
The butcher's son is not a part-time burglar.
The staff at the local Indian are not
high as kites – seeing dragons in every bowl of rice –
and it's not even nine o'clock.
The daffodil bulbs are not stabbing each other underground,
jostling and pushing to come up first – no.
Nothing is happening, and it's happening
right here.

No tourists have arrived without maps
in order to find themselves.
No two people are lying to each other.
No one is looking in a mirror hoping to find their youth.
No one is stood outside the chippy trying to think themselves thin.
No one called Marvin is about to divulge the secrets of his sock
   drawer.

No one in the pub is drinking to forget to drink the truth in.
No one and nothing is happening at all – least of all to
Sally and Rupert Entwhistle of 2 Chestnut Crescent who have recently
adopted an egg sandwich called Jim.

Nothing. Happens. Forever.
It takes up all the space we would like to swap for something.
None of the cows in the field are full of milk, their udders
heavy with emptiness.
No one is lip-reading this to a man who sells beach brollies.
No tic-tac man in a small un-numbered office is
counting the days to when he won't have to. Count.
No one is packing a suitcase, writing a note,
preparing to leave no one for some other no one.
No one is hoping for a child by this time next year –
one they don't know yet, but who'll have their eyes.
No one up a ladder is wondering how they got there.
No one knows what causes spring to begin –
one thing to end, another to start.

No one is falling in or out of love.
No one is raising a glass to the future, saying, *this time next year…*
No one is brushing a tear away.
No one is cocking a snook at the past.
No one and nothing is happening at all.
And mostly none of it is happening,
right here.

Billy

Billy at the cemetery oversees the dead.
He counts them in.
He counts them out.
He hates their quiet arrival.
He hates the way the women refuse to marry him.
He hates the way the men refuse to be friends.
He keeps all this under his hat.
But, the staff know.
Billy hates the dead.
The way they don't fight back.
Let him walk all over them.
Their voices that hang from the trees like nooses.
The queer open mouth of the cemetery gates.
He stands guard at night in case more ghosts
slip out than he's bargained for.
He has banned all hilarity, all levity from the place.
He removes all the special tokens people leave.
Windmills. Teddy bears. Footballs.
They all go missing.
One grin as you pass his office
and you're dead meat.
The men at the council love Billy.
'As far as we're concerned he has a job for life.
He's taken the job so seriously –
why, he's almost dead himself.
That's attention to detail, that is.'
People are always dying to meet him.
Everyone loves Billy.

Second-hand Men

She likes her men second-hand.
Once they've been bedded in,
she finds they're a better fit, are easier on the skin,
more to her throwaway taste.
Also, once she gets them home
they seem to know their place, as if
by instinct. Like a dog.
Some of them circle their baskets a little warily
at first, but sleep claims them finally.
If the woolly-moth edges of their dreams disturb her,
she has a door she can shut.

She likes her men well road-tested.
The tyres with a bit of grip.
The headlamps still jaunty. The bumper can be damaged, but
at least that smell of new car is all gone
from his breath. (And that card on the dashboard
from the blonde he met in Ipswich.
She would only have been good for him.)

You have to shop around, she says, so
these days she is careful.
Especially if they own more than one full socket set.
She likes them to forget all the places they were going.
She makes sure they don't remember all the places
that she's been.
She's either on the piste, or the sunbed, or the rebound.
She's a woman of distinction with no identifying marks.
Her passport belongs to someone she once knew.

(But, I digress –)
She checks them over for that over-garaged look.
Always makes sure they can be jump-started, and
that way, there's no harm done;

because it's a shame to waste when
there's such a lot of wear left in them. They wash up so well.
No one would ever guess.

And they're often so grateful,
they'll do anything for you. Well, almost anything.
They won't love you. She doesn't expect miracles.
She knows they've had that knocked out of them
years ago.

Home Town

This is his home town only because
he doesn't know how to leave.
The way out involves time-tables.
He has trouble with them.
This is his home town.
This is where he cleans his teeth.
Like a bruise, he is not sure how he got here.
Just that he is here.
He offers strangers crisps.

He stands at train stations
looking at maps.
Eyes as big as gob-stoppers.
'Skegness, it's so bracing,' the poster says.
He wonders where it is.
Once he went to Leeds but
he kept his eyes shut and so
the memory is blurred.
He has come to call for Peter.
Peter is his mentor, rides ladies' bikes
and thinks he's from the moon.

We ask him where he's from, he says
a hospital in Middlesbrough.
His mother had him there because of Aunty Sadie
and her breeding dogs like.
He's never known his dad.
It seemed the best for all concerned.
Though sometimes on his birthday
he wonders if he's dead.

This is his home town, his I'm-in-chains-
grown-cold town.
He used to be a window cleaner, but
didn't like heights.
He could only do the bottom ones and people
can be funny. Now
he works at the bookies but has never seen a horse.
He stands and watches trains.
Watches people boarding them
and offers strangers crisps.

Lazarus Enrolls at the Gym

Maybe I had no business there,
but it felt good.
After all that other nonsense
I needed to feel alive again.

The first thing they queried was the stick.
Then
I could tell the eye-patch hadn't gone down well
either. The blonde whiskey on reception
is sent to check insurance procedure;

that's when one of my bandages
(I still keep them for old times' sake)
starts to unravel.
Things could be going better. When
the arm he assured me would be steady as a rock
falls off,
they're watching me through the toning room
window, and I can't tell if
they're laughing or crying.
Both, I think.
Sometimes I wonder why he didn't just leave well alone.
Now, they whisper about me on street corners.
The smart money at the temple is always on me
to stay the course or die in the attempt.
'Look, he's the guy who made the comeback,' they point.
'Or maybe he's just a heavy sleeper?' Roars of laughter.
Why did he have to interfere?
The cave was paid for.
As far as the act was concerned,
Martha and Mary were always the better singers. Anyways,
the bugle was never the same after Jericho.
Thank God the treadmill machine goes off without incident.
When I leave, the girl passes me a discreet carrier
for the arm.
Asks me if I'd like to introduce a friend.
'Sure' I say – 'Okay if he brings his own bed?'

The Back of Beyond

You can't see the sunset
for well-meaning druids
and ex bank managers from Croydon
busy cooking hedgehogs – and women
weaving their own sandals and reading
Tarot Cards.
(You know who you are.)

So many folk now live in the
Back of Beyond.
(I won't be specific. I think you'll see why.)
Moon-paving your driveway
is tricky now that
all the best moon pavers have
moved back to London.
The old pathway to
the Saints Holy Well
is bristling with walkers in
hair-shirts and trainers
and strange loping dogs with
questionable smiles.
There is bunting across the old pasture
and a festival to someone remarkable, pagan
and wildly anonymous, every third day.

There is also a hat shop, a tea shop, a map shop.
Beyond's on the way up
there's no doubt about it.
The lane down here was heaving with crystals and runes
and a man wearing spoons. You can laugh, but
I heard tell of a miracle up on 'THE' hill of
a man who by all reports had been ILL.

They say he built a tandem
using just wire and the discarded teeth of sheep.
They say he muttered of junk food
and cried Woking in his sleep.

But he's better now, he's dead.
It was his wish to be recycled and so he will be.
He's being replanted as I write.
Is it too soon to talk of relics and possible Zen outlets
for the more discerning?

Tell me, have I been too specific?

The Test

My father's optimism on driving
was immense.
As big as a Rolls Royce.
A lifetime's ambition.
All vehicles would be his at last.
King of the Road. Top Dog.
A highway he could take
beyond himself.

At 83, with failing sight,
a walking stick
and crumbling heart –
he offered to take your old car
off your hands.
'A few simple lessons,' he said,
all he'd need really.
'Maybe – just the one.'

Enlightenment

The Master says
I must recognise myself by
the plume of smoke that rises from the heart.
Outside the window
a bird is teaching me about nothing.
On the doorstep
a cat tutors in what may be achieved
tomorrow.
There are two purple cranes
eyeing me from the red roof.
In the attic, my teacher awaits me.
He prescribes caution, for everyone.
Except me.
For me he advises bedlam
in large quantity.
He instructs that, for me, there should
and will be chaos.
You, he says, must become the mad dog, the fool,
the blind flautist, the crazy crone, the leper.
You must live alone in the mountains.
The higher, the better.
When you are tired, still you must go on.
When you are mute and have forgotten speech –
still you will not have been there long enough.
After death, you must even be your own ghost.
'And you,' I ask, 'you, great Master, will you visit me?
Will you come to me disguised as a sandstorm,
at my moment of enlightenment?'
'No,' he says. 'You will have your flute and your
tame rock, that is known as Eric. And why would I
visit a crazy person when my gifts are needed here?'
'You are too kind Master,' I said.
Just before
reaching up, and pushing him off the roof.

Timothy

Timothy the tapir –
from the first we were obsessed with him,
only ever saw the best of him.
His fine black, piggish eyes,
his elegant snout, his rapier tapir wit –
for us, these all held clout.
We cocked a snook at neighbours,
walked him at all hours with
our heads held high.

We took him here, we took him there, then
as a special treat – to the theatre, late last June.
From the first he seemed at home.
He ate ice cream with no spoon,
which caused a mild sensation;
he left a present in the aisle, with dramatic presentation.
He had such flair, he had such style,
you can see how struck we were.

And then.

You might say you saw it coming – his
flaws, his faults began to show.
He wore sequins, ostrich feathers;
he became quite ostentatious.
In his top hat, suit and tails
he said he felt he had a calling, that
he loved wildly all things thespian.

So, we talked it through till dawn with him
and we said it would be hard for a tapir
aiming for
an equity-type card, and
did he know the hours were long, were cruel?

Could he chat up the director, and
could he live in lonely digs?
But he hardly seemed to listen.
Gave a sort of Mona Lisa smile and said,
just nipping out for cigs…

And there our tapir story ends, for friends, we've not seen Timothy
from that June day to now –
he never phones, he never writes; at the
pub quiz, he is missing,
Then TODAY, a card from the Alhambra People's Theatre, Yarmouth
saying: just a small role – Oscar Wilde (the handbag).
Thanks for being spiffing.

Town People on a Beach

are edgy fledglings.
Fledgy edglings.
They are not sure what the sea is.
They wait for some sort of official introduction –
some kind of salty handshake.
They hold their breath in, nervously,
and puff their cheeks out a lot.
They smoke a lot, even those who've given up.
They stand awkwardly in grey socks.
(Bare feet was something Man Friday did.)
They crush coke cans.
They bark louder than the dog they're with.
The dog runs in circles.
He craves Acacia Avenue, Billericay Bungalows.
The clean crisp smell of them. The dry apple safety.
The dogs' barks and the people's barks circle each other.
The people put shells to their ears – and straightaway
hear the sound of the tube, the toot of taxis.
The sound of feet caressing pavement.
A tear escapes them.

Not for them wave-dunking or seaweed-scrying.
'Vicious bastards, beaches,' I hear one of them say,
and another, a mother this time:
'Put that sea down, you don't know where it's been.'
Then. You can see them.
They are heading for the end of the pier,
for the kiss-me-quick hats, the candy floss,
the bearded lady, the man with two heads in the hall of mirrors;
anything normal.
There they stand with their gleaming steaming bags of chips.
What makes me so sure? How do I know?

Fancy a chip?

Silver Wedding

You can't miss it.
The house is called Dun-Trying.
They are a little afraid of the voices in the wind.
The things that stand untouched
but rattling in the sideboard.
He had always known her.
They met in the schoolyard – it was
easy at first sight.
All the family liked her.
So he married. All of them.
The house groaned under the weight.
For years now, he's been missing –
presumed found.

They are two bank statements pulling together.
Once, he would have liked to have travelled,
to have kept snakes, something different.
Now his own venom when they speak is enough.
They smoke different pipes, at night in separate
armchairs. They sleep in separate rooms –
her bed is a hundred years old, it has seen death.
His is a new hammock slung each night in the garden.
Even in their dreams they avoid eye-contact.
Her hands are spiders' webs; his are pale as the moon.

On each anniversary
they recoil from something more of themselves.
Their amnesia almost total.
Each kiss an anaesthetic, deepening.
Something in the sideboard, grinning, rattling.

Good Advice

So much goes unheeded.

Never speak to a stranger.
Never drink white milk on a black night.
Never drink a whole night in one glass.
Never offer a stranger a black night.
Never wear a vest.

Never wear the vest of a stranger.
Never change your face when the wind does.
But always change your vest, when
you speak to the wind (this is polite).
But never speak to a stranger who wears the wind.
Or, your face.

If only I'd listened.
I remember it all.

Never tell stories you can't keep.
Never keep promises you can't break.
Never count your chickens and never iron cats,
but always iron your socks as this keeps cats out –
and never wear green unless you know
where the full moon's been. Unless it's a Friday,
and then you're alright.
Never believe your dad when he's had a drink and
never bet on the same horse as your Uncle Pat and
never risk the fish (unless it's a rabbit).
Never wear shoes that are smaller than a dachshund,
and never believe in the length of the bed
or the strength of garage walls.
Never look a gift mouth in the horse.
Never cross the road while wearing a salt cellar.
Never go on a blind date with someone you know.

If only I'd listened.
I remember it all.
Never shelter under a storm when a tree is raging.

Never listen to people who give good advice.

Neil, Honey

Never go first when landing on the moon.
Why?
Because there were no pictures of Neil,
poor old Neil –
basking in his own reflection of himself
taking a picture of the others.

When he got home
and his mum asked for a look at the snaps –
and his gran asked too –
wanting to show off with them down at the
local burger and mugging joint –
what could he say?
'You silly astronaut,' they said.
'All that way, and not so much as a Polaroid –
Neil, honey, what were you thinking of?'

So.
Take a tip from Neil and his mum.
Never go first when landing on the moon.

Making Ends Meet

He is American.
She is Russian.
They will be making an arrangement on the internet.
He is called John.
John's house is big.
He has a room prepared for her there.
She has a smile designed for him.
She will be Anna Karenina to his Davy Crockett. If
he is fool enough
and
she is shrewd enough
neither of them will win.
Their children will be burger-eating ballet dancers.
They will not thank them in either language,
but will be confused in both.
They will all become tall and gangly with the strain.
They will move to Switzerland and hoover lawns and small dogs.
Reissa and John will grow cold together.
Everything that is crazy and terrible can be bought.
The ways of avoiding truth are difficult and dangerous
but perseverance is its own reward.

The Dog in the Painting

Once he was all dog –
muddy paws, stick in the mouth,
flip-flop tail.
Now he is all seaweed.
But.
He wears it well, this sea-change.
Still chases the stick of himself
back to its source.
His round galoshes eyes are all ocean.
His heart inside a thousand shells.
So many journeys awaited him.

This painter-woman removes him.
Paints him out of the picture,
all because he was the wrong dog.
They didn't want dogs spoiling the view,
so, he must go. He is gone.
He was a temporary dog only.
A dog for a day.
Just as he had felt the bright diamonds of sand
beneath his feet,
licked the salt from his running paws
beside the child that is laughing
while flying a kite –
just as he smelled the air full with the coming storm,
pricked his ears at the sound of his own good luck –
he felt the green liquid from her brush washing over him.
The painter-woman
erasing his short life with a few short strokes.
'I am a million dogs,' he wants to say.
'You and your kind cannot win here.'
Inside himself
the beauty of a green field. Unravelling.

Sundays

Dear Father and God and all them Saints –
well here I am again,
looking at you through the small window,
you being the head guy here and all
and I've just this minute now come from the street where
they don't like me.
No, none of the bastards like me.
Sorry for swearing this early on and all, but
to tell the truth, and sister says you should always tell the truth –
the truth being that they bloody well hate me. Never mind don't
   like me.

Except for that weekend when I'd got new roller-skates that is, and
Dad said he could see it coming, and Mam said it was just an excuse
and that trouble was brewing and the skates were frigged, sorry,
   broken.
Now, just now, I got another fist right in my back
and all I'm doing is walking down the god damn street – sorry
(and I ask for forgiveness for all the swearing, especially the
   swearing I haven't done yet
better to be sorry than safe and that.) Father, any chances of a hand
   here,
because, I just done like God in that temple that time,
when he upturns the lot of them for playing poker and stuff,
and throws them all clean down some steps
(I've always liked that part Father, I don't know about you...)
but I appear to have given two of them a
right thumping – and god I enjoyed it – could you
forgive me in the name of the Father and of the Son and the Holy
   Goat, and
could the penance not be 'to go' Father, because unless there's a
   back way out of here
the two of them are waiting outside for me.
So much for Sundays, eh Father?

Message

Dear both,
Eileen called. You were out.
Wonder why? Ha-ha.
I have left the banjo in the fridge
and scraped off most of the cheesecake.
The woman was seeing red.
Jesus. I was scared I don't mind telling you.
And her plaster cast only just off on the
Thursday.

She says – 'I see Paddy McGinty is away back to
his old she-goat.' (Apparently, that's you, Sinead.)
Ha-double-ha.
And why no rent left for me in usual place,
while I think of same?
No-bloody-ha-at-all-ha.
Am living on fresh air and ciggies here.
Can you not have some decency?
Did I not get you the phone number of
Christy Moore's ex brother-in-law?

Anyway, Eileen says she'll see both of you in Hell
before the band's left to youse two's
cheating bastards. And no,
I don't know where she got the goat.
He only answers to 'Will you move your arse ye eejut,
before I move it for ye.'
I'm lying. He answers to bugger all.
Keep your frigging paws off that last piece of cheesecake.
See you in Hell – yours (the other cheating bastard)
Eithne Cecilia Cavanagh, your
ever-loving landlady.

— from *Zuzu's Petals* (2007) —

The Chocolate Girls

They live near me, the chocolate girls
with their chocolate curls
and their hazelnut whirl come-hither smiles.
They are steeped in chocolate from nine to five.
They are Cleopatra, Mata Hari and Scheherazade.
No man escapes from the chocolate girls.

They leave on bikes, they leave on foot.
It's all a rush at the factory gates.
They've all got dates, they can't be late.
Strawberry skin and caramel hearts within.
White chocolate hair, Malibu fudge and nougat flesh,
picking the kids up from the crèche.
They are steeped in chocolate from six to ten then
they ride chocolate bikes home
before starting again. No man can escape them,
their marshmallow eyes and mind-bright souls.
No one knows what's in their minds,
only that chocolate has made them this way.
Some are sweet, some are mysterious;
some lie in pyramids, others in gold and silver tissue.
If you try to break them, more will come.
Chocolate is in their blood.
At night they sleep in cocoa pod houses.
By day the thick cracknel of their lives is melted down,
the chocolate girls that live near me.

Children's Games

And it's always just like that.
You have to swallow a piece of gum or a part of a clock
and not be seen to be sick or bothered –
or wallop a wild cat with a dead dog's leg and if it scratches you
and you get rabies you have to cross yourself six times
behind the priest's back and then you'll live forever. Maybe.
And then you have to
nick half a coconut from the fair
AND spit on the shadow of the man who
does the waltzers whose wife has a beard and sits in the tent
telling fortunes where if you hear what she's said, even one word –
you'll grow an extra foot, or an extra arm – or both –
and you'll be like old Crutchy Miller that lost his with the gangrene.
And it's always just like that.

And then you have to
touch the mad nun's skirt and run quick as hell
past Jimmy the Tramp who used to be a darts player
until the slings and arrows of the world got to him –
just like mam says they got to dad.
And it's always, always, just like that.
Then.
You have to run away from home and live rough in
a tent on the big skip where people say
there once was a murder, and then you have to breeze back
in at home and ask: 'so what's for tea?' – and not cry if
they didn't even notice you was gone.

Then.
You have to walk real calm and lay your head down
like a Sunday offering on the railway-lines –
and leave it there, and leave it there, and leave it there – until
someone with ginger hair and muddy trousers goes past
(and it's got to be BOTH, just one doesn't count)
and they shout: 'Hey Mad Nellie One Eye – get yourself home
your tea's on't table fresh from't chippie. And – is it true they've
 taken back your telly?'

And then you've got to run all't way home and unless – and only IF –
your mam's dead, not tell anyone that you've locked your cousin
in her dad's allotment shed –
BUT – if your mam's dead –
you can let on after tea.
And it's always, always, just like that.

And IF they ask,
and even if you're not scared like Jimmy Cagney wasn't in that film
where his friend the priest begs him and all –
and he dies pretending to squirm and be a rat –
don't let on about none of it.
Except if absolutely EVERYONE in the world is dead.

And then you can only own up to the coconut.

When Dad was Father Christmas

It was great.
For two weeks of the year
he got to pretend he was Fred McMurray.
Blown in off one of those New York streets
like some kindly hobo
to do only good and put the world to rights.
All twinkling eyes and white beard.
The beard fitted the second he put it on.
Even the red coat knew him.
Had just been waiting to be worn.
'No one's really sure where I'm from,' he whispered.
'A magic castle at Coney Island
or maybe a bench in Central Park. Who's to say?'

Lots of Judy Garlands and Mickey Rooneys
sat on his knee.
The queue stretched all the way
down forty-first and forty-second street.
Ginger Rodgers and Fred Astaire
danced to entertain the queue and Liz Taylor rode in
on National Velvet and asked could she have her own pony.
Please. And rode home on it.
Jimmy Cagney gave dad a bullet-proof life just
for those two weeks.

And, for those two weeks, things were different.
We were all of us happy. Crazy and happy.
And, I thought, maybe wishes do come true
and the world will be okay.
There were kids' expectant faces everywhere.
We can all of us be anything we want to be.
The ice in the park will hold up under the skater's weight.
There will be a banner that reads Happy New Year.
And it will be.

But like in all good movies,
the director decides enough is enough.
And the snow machine gets turned off.
And the children look down and see how big they got.
And cracks appear in the ice again.
And the queue to see Santa gets smaller and smaller.
Until it's just one little kid who wants to become a priest.
And the reindeer gets an offer of steady work down Tucson way.
And Lenny and Ed dismantle the grotto.
And a Bette Davis look-alike moves in – selling her cheap wigs and bourbon-filled chocolates. All lip-curl and bad breath.
And they move Dad out.

When he gets home I hang his coat up,
then we lay his beard to rest,
and he sinks down in his old armchair
like a sad King Canute.
I know then it's all over.
Even the street cars, with their little lights of hope,
have all been swallowed up.
And I fish down inside his pocket and find one last wish-list.
And it says 'I wish it could be Christmas every day.'

And I know whose list it is.

The Apple House

The bones of the old house
stand on an orchard. So,
the bones and blood of my house
are apples. Whole juicy crinolines of them.
Here the trees are laden, are ladies with ruby fans
pulpy with apple segments. Their fans speak
the language of apples.
I speak the language of trees, of apples.

I myself, though you cannot see it, am apple.
My fingertips are apple pips.
My blood runs clear as cider blood.
In the night the bricks rustle
like the soft leaves of russets nestled at dawn
as they protect the ground from itself.
The earth has a way of answering fruit.
It is the swing of a pendulum as time itself becomes edible.
Over my dreams birds fly, call to me:
'You are not alone. Let the tree that loves you ripen.'

The birds protect the apple shell
of my head on the pillow.
Our eyes watch the leaning towers of trees
sway in the wind, the long branches
of people's dreams,
the green skin of them unpeeling,
unravelling behind their swollen eyes.

We are turning, turning into
the red pulse of ourselves as we wake.
Our teeth close on the creamy, unbitten day.

Then.
We are falling. Fallen.
Our throats swollen with autumn.
The years pour through our bodies
like cool, silky, green water.
Our bodies that are sinking are
the crumpling of flesh. Only that.
I am wearing my dream skin now, do you see?

Like the centre of the fruit we have dreamed ourselves.
Like the centre of fruit, we are ticking flesh.
We are the perfumed, opal core of apples.
Within me the apples that are golden hang.
My apple soul at last comes home.

Head

My mother's lighter head has arrived
and we carry her upstairs, until
her heavier head returns.

The room becomes a sea of mints, eau-de-cologne,
half-eaten biscuits, bottles of glycerine,
tinctures, rubs and linaments to rub
the other head away with. A pride
of hot water bottles stalk the room, between
the layers of her covers and the tangerine-
striped walls.
The temperature of the room is uncertain.
It struts from tropical to arctic.
There are two kettles, one for use and one for show.
We must only let in part of the light, when we enter.

A priest calls by, blesses a small candle
which we light together. It is the feast of All Souls.
Mother sleeps.
A social worker calls next and discusses her after-care
on a mobile phone. (After-care involves out and about.)
My mother's official (officially light) head spits
venomous remarks into the mobile phone.
The social worker leaves in search of her own after-care;
her own head neither light nor heavy. It clings ferociously
to her clipboard-laden shoulders and buzzes like the phone.

Outside the small window, where her lilac tree stands,
where my taller tree stood, before the winds shook it –
I can almost still see it, believe where it was there will
be spring again,
see the two nestled together, brushing each other softly down
as around them mist is falling.

I watch my father pace the path below looking
for my mother's head.
(We are hoping the head will see sense.)
We hang around the house, just breathing; we
are both of us in the later stages of breathing.
There is a knock at the door, a box is delivered.
Neither of us can look at it, it lies unopened.
The sound of it, its rhythmic breathing, is the flurry
of birds, many birds, settling, then finally unsettling.

Strange Meeting

You always hurried me on past them.
The crazy twins.
We always knew where we would meet them,
by the beck – hubble bubble, toil and trouble –
and that they would be jabbering in their
crazy talk, with just those two heads
to hold the one thought.

All in white, with weird aprons, heavy boots
and red patchwork bonnets.
You walked on their side in case they lashed out at us.
I remember their eyes were livid blue
like bruised bluebells and that
their skin was white like
no blood flowed in their veins at all.
They had plaits to their waists
with bright red ribbons
that flapped in the icy tinker's wind.
Their voices were shrill – old kettles
hissing over wild flames.
They had one walk between them.
They had one destination and one eye on it.
'It's a shame,' you always said,
when we were safe at home and sitting by
our different fire. And sadness came.

And I remembered how they steered each other
like two wild ponies but
without looking. How they flew
across the beck, so much quicker than us.
Queens of the night-time blue-black air.
The heavy boots making no sound.
The singing kettle in their lungs hanging
in the winter dark.

The Space Around

In the space that surrounds apples – there is a hint of banana
In the space that surrounds elephants – there is a hint of pyjama

In the space around ribs – there is a hint of spare
In the space around this poem – a lion's lair
In the space round summer flesh – a hint of bare

In the space around small – the hint of a giant frog, just hopped
In the space around hippies – the sound of a talking log
In the space on the hairdresser's floor – the scent of hair, just cropped

In the space around mothers – there is a hint of a vest
In the space around the bottom of the class – the cry, 'I did my best'

In the space around Finnan – a hint of haddock
In the space around Johnny – a suggestion of Craddock

In the space around footballers – a hint of blondes
In the space around Harry Potter – a hint of wands

In the space around clocks – the hint of lost time
In the space around nuns – just the hint of crime

In the space around haiku – a hint of things in blossom
In the space around bridges – a hint of ghosts trying to cross them

In the space around daydreams – a hint of truth
In the space around a man's wrinkles – small pockets of youth

In the space around coats – the scent of going
In the space around death – a cloud of unknowing

In the space around loneliness – the fear of the unknown
In the space around spare rooms – the sound of children, flown

In the space around tomorrow – the memory of today
In the space around old houses – distant voices, gone away

In the space around graves – the hint of things still left to say
In the space around your heartache – a love that won't wash away

In the space around shells – the murmur of the sea
In the space around you – always – a hint of me

The Blue Cooker

In the kitchen
an old man is cooking on an old blue cooker.

The cooker is in love with all things Spanish.
It wants to feast its taste buds on a Galician extravaganza.
It wants to wear ricotta next to its skin. Real ricotta.
It wants to burn with the flames of flamenco.
It craves passion.
It never wants to see a ready meal for one again.
Not to mention sardines.

My name is Conchita-pancetta-paella
rioja-peperonata-Gonzalez, it croons.
It makes little whinnying noises
like those Spanish academy horses.
It is imagining kicking off its dull saggy casters,
popping on a pair of soft, black, leather
clicking shoes, that click, and click and click
against the hard kitchen floor.
It would die to have its own fan.

It imagines the coquettish turn of its head
behind such a fan.
It begins to rock softly on its moorings.
Just the thought of it.
The old man looks puzzled.
Checks the bit of newspaper under the wonky leg.
Goes to turn the gas off, and then
IT happens.

He doesn't know why, but he begins to sing.
Imagines he is a wild gypsy soloist.
Serenades the sad blue eyes of the cooker. His voice soars high
   above the kitchen
out into the dizzying spell of the night sky.
The cooker is as wild as he.
Its castanets are on fire.
Its mock-replica-all-purpose-hood-with-dual-attachments
has become detached.

'This is IT,' it cries. 'This is where my life really begins!
This is freedom – this is beauty – this is SPAIN!!!'
And the old man and the cooker
embrace and are happy.
Together they dance.

Children's Hospice

She calls it 'the dining room'. I hear 'the dying room'.
The next room is the 'rainbow suite'.
Through the window the garden is exquisite.
The ends of children's smiles lie at the foot of each bed.
The pillows are smooth as truth can make them.

There is a liquid grief that pierces the vein
and punctures the heart.

Sliding on the shiny floors,
tearing pages out of books,
breaking toys are named activities.
Here, where the future casts no shadow save its own,
train sets stand idle.
Small houses with make-believe telephones
that do not ring are next to the games box.
A hundred games with so many lucky endings
that will never be opened.

Inside each parent
a desert is whistling in the mind's oasis,
a scream is wandering, of pain and anger.
Whether to have flowers or not.
What small hands the clock on the wall has.
Inside each parent's mind another scene is forming where
the endless fountain pours tiger-lily water,
where the green eye of the desert God favours them.
And the ship is sent back. The child is taken home
and grief is just a word for someone else in mind.
No clothes await disposal.
No special pictures on the mantelpiece.

All the time we are walking through the rainbow suite
those who went missing join us.
In every corner of the room, small handprints on the paperwork.
They will not wash away.
The chimera of colours spills from inside each.
The green eye of the desert God is insistent.

The York Floods

My city is floating. It seemed like fun at first.
We have been to Clifford's Tower
to watch the ducks. We have watched geese
walking down Coney Street.
We put flippers on our feet
and divers' helmets on and went fishing
in a boat in Fulford village.
We caught a strange merman and did not throw him back.
The grass and the sky and the water
hold our reflections up to heaven.
Water is singing in the heart of York.
We pretend to be dolphins
and swim alongside a bus heading for the station.
There are thousands of people skimming stones
across the submerged city that is halted.
We run like penguins down the steep incline
of the shimmering allotments.
We are bold as reeds by the banks of the Nile.
The water is rising even more.
Maybe this water world will not end – so,
we hold each other's hands tighter now.
Is our city gone? Is a city under water still alive?
We hold each other's hands.
What is the city whispering?
A last boat arrives. We do not board it.
We caught a strange merman and did not throw him back.

Be Careful

'Be careful of the tiles,' he said.
'I just laid them.'
They were new kitchen tiles.
They would give our small kitchen
a new lease of life – overlooking the neighbours' garden
brimming with dead cats and rotting prams.
The neighbours who threw a brick at my head, and almost killed me.
The neighbours who set fire to my house, drunk as skunks.
The neighbours who chopped down my mother's lilac tree for fun.
I won't go on.
I'm sure you get the picture.

I can see Dad now,
stooped over those red and yellow tiles
like some massive chess game he was playing.
I can see Mam now,
sat with her head in her hands,
wondering what our next move should be.
Our walls still black from the smoke. The hot stink of it.

'Be careful,' Dad said.
'That's all I ask.'

Tortoises

Please stop putting tortoises through my letterbox.
I do not wish to buy anything from your range of
tortoise hair colourants – interesting as
the range is.
Nor will I be joining Terry the tortoise at meditation class
next Tuesday Week.
I am not wanting to buy any frozen tortoises or
take delivery of kebab specials of same.
Frankly – and I pin my colours to the mast here,
I am neutral vis-à-vis the tortoise situation.
While I may have indicated my willingness to vote for
your in-house tortoise candidate at the last election,
since then I have had some of the straw and guano
removed from my eyes.
I am now in favour of the eco-tortoise candidate,
though I no longer wish to provide board and lodgings
for his fellow party-snorers.
Mainly because it would take at least three days
to get them all to their rooms.
I fear on your part, you are taking the lettuce
out of what was a genuine offer.
So, please. Cease with the ringing of the doorbell
and leaving two of them on the doorstep.
It lacks dignity for all concerned.
Be warned. I am the proud owner of a terrapin
who answers to Tarquin.
Sir, he is armed.

The Point of Men

Like mountains they are simply there –
awaiting climbing.
With their unexpected hand-holds
beckoning.
With their hinterlands and base-camps.
(That suggestive planting of flags.)
With their my-wife-doesn't-understand-me
glaciers.
Tread carefully here.
The ice on these is thinner than you think.
The most difficult face is always
the one you must conquer.
The one that beat all previous attempts –
and foiled the rescue teams.
What do we gain?
They stand loftily eyeing us from a distance.
The nearer we get, through wind and rain
and snow – the more the point of them is lost
to sight.
But still we rope up, buy provisions.
Feel ecstatic at the thought of touching sun and sky.

Full Fruit Salad

Dear Peach,
I would like to be strawberry
to your cream.
You are grapes I note
(but not of wrath, I hope).
Myself, I have been tangerine too long.
I am keen to apricot with you
as am quite fresh and luscious
at present moment.

Your old kiwi
has snuggled up with new banana
(or so I hear…)
Are you a man or a mandarin?

My lychees await your quick response.

Dear Rucksack

I cannot understand why you are so heavy.
I cannot understand why you are so leaden.
Today you are shedding baroque tears.
I've done everything I can for you.
I have taken you to several traditional restaurants.
You have eaten pumpkin soup with truffles.
A traditional gypsy has played to you.
You have been fed chocolate cake with sweet almond sauce.
You have loitered in dark doorways in medieval Prague.
You have walked where the Golem walks.
You have seen the oldest bed of the Hapsburg in Vienna.
You have seen the toilet of Franz Joseph –
the one with the little blue horses on.

You have sat on the birthing chair of the Duchess of Duval
who was buried with her favourite horse.
You have been trampled underfoot on the Viennese Underground.
You have been locked in the Hungarian Parliament due to a chefs'
    convention.
You have been asked to leave an art gallery and a Strauss waltz evening
for fear you were a security risk.
You have inadvertently been left on a funicular in Budapest.
But, I came back for you.
So, why so queasy?
Like me, do you yearn for Heathrow –
and the complete lack of mosaics, marble, and chandeliers
in the toilets?

In My Day

These days (forgive me)
you are a little crazy when I visit you.
You say that last night
there were sheep in the ward, and that
the people with them
meant you no harm and that
they were kind in their bleating
and ushered
you back to bed, safe as a lamb.

Before I go, we laugh about it all
and together we
round the last few up.
'Still,' you say.
'It wouldn't have been allowed
once upon a time. Not in my day.'

Donor

When I am gone
I would like my organs used well.
I would like my paintings of flowers
and gardens and butterflies
used as bombs and cannon shot.
I would like my laughter used as rapid gunfire.
I would like my arthritic bones used as
battering rams in any remaining no-go areas.

I would like my best day ever, when I almost
made it as a human being, used
as the breakthrough grounds for a peace treaty.

I would like my stories and my poems
inserted into the hearts of politicians, and
I would like my belief that
there is a better way forward for us all
left as an explosive package
in every rail and bus station in the country.
When I am gone, these are my wishes.

Not too much to ask for, surely?

How to Spot a Poet

Watch out for them.
The ones who say they're not poets, not really.
Watch out for the things they say they do
especially
the ones whose real job is body-doubling for corpses
or deep-sea diving to catch fish fingers and fat rascals
or flower-arranging for harmless dictators
or ten-pin bowling with false eyes buried inside golf balls
or listening to Mozart through keyholes using only a thimble
or carrying temporary bus stop signs into mobile libraries
under cover of midnight
or painting themselves bright green and howling like a giraffe under
    a full moon
or sharpening the second best quill pen that ever belonged to Byron.
Watch out for the poets who are not really poets.
Watch out for the flicker of rage in their eyes.
Watch out for the jobs they say they do at the edge of the wood
    that they almost
have invented – and don't be fooled by
any of them.

The Other House

When the pain comes and my warrior legs
grow tired –
I go to live in the other house.
The one with roses round the door,
such strange roses as I never saw before.
Huge and apricot, falling over themselves
at their own beauty, their own sound.
I hold my breath and listen to them.
A thousand golden butterflies make up the door
of this, my other house.
They beat inside my simple heart and remind me
that I too can fly.

Here, the day is as long as I wish, and here
no pain dare enter – I care not to let it enter.
Why, I want to ask, may I not always walk
within this green place?
A voice there answers:
'Child, for as long as you can bear that warrior world,
this other house will be your refuge and your salvation.
A place will be kept for you that knows no walls.'
And the butterflies that were the open door, sang.
And the flowers, so amazed at their own joy, opened up and spoke
    saying:
'Where the rose itself walks, so shall you.
Weep no more, for always this best of houses waits for you.'
And I wept no more.
And within the light of day I walked again.

— from *The Ruby Slippers* (2011) —

Quiet Auditorium

Outside, the snow is singing –
there is a knock at the door.
I open it, you are there,
eyes dark-rimmed and solemn round.
I know half of you has stood
there before. You speak snatched words
in the weasel-sharp wind. Outside
an animal is bleeding, you say. You
require a room to rest in, just
to catch your breath, to
have a seat by a fire and
perhaps food – be no trouble, no trouble,
before moving on again. Your Spartan
mood unsettles me. I close
my splintered eyes to think –
and opening them, look up to see the heavy
door shut fast. So, the problem is solved

but
what was it, what was I about to say? My
hands are cold, blancmange-like, my heart
is a small box,
wired. Inside the room I can
see a young woman sat reading, while
through the windows, prickly-steamed,
an animal is warming itself
at the fire. A snow coat forms around me.
Outside, the snow is taking its seat, ready
for the next act, but
it must wait for your cue. Hush –
there is a knock at the door;
get up, get up and put this page down
now,
for it is your door.

On Wearing My Uncle Patrick's Hat

I wonder
how many times did my Uncle's hat
glimpse this old lane?
On his way to Aunt Rose's house perhaps –
the one that got bombed?
Or even halfway round the city walls
on the Whit-Walk,
sat like a jaunty owl on his head.
Later, the hat became my fathers' hat.
It sat on his head like a raven on the wing.
The wearing of hats to him, always
a thing of mystery.
The hat saw both of them
home from two wars.
It heard talk of a boat to America.
It heard of work to be had and street after
street of Irish good luck
for the taking.
It saw itself Top of the World.
It imagined a brave new beginning.
Now, I wear the hat –
out in the old lane just a stone's throw
from Rose's.
The ruins of the house.
The secrets of the hat.
I analyse the dust of them both.
They fit me, perfectly.

The Grenz

Trees, hundreds of them,
slim warriors, leaf-bright blades –
between two of them, he saw
the smallest face.
They were on the Grenz, the border.

To this smallest, frightened face
(that looked from behind the border
that was trees) he made a sign.
My father made the sign of the cross,
called out: 'You have found a friend
in the trees.' (He imparts good news slowly,
with a King's air, still does.) 'How many are you?'
he asked – the voice returned to him, 'forty.'

To take the wrong track at the border
is easily done. So, he must take them
the longest route, but the safe one.
Through the thickest of the forest
they flitted, his own collection of butterflies,
to freer soil.

It was dark before they parted, at midnight.
Crossing over, the last of them
turned, made his own sign of the cross to
a face between the trees, a young soldier.
Leaving its shape there, in the wind, just
above his head – a benediction on the front
that chance returned to them their souls.
'How many are you?' The wind returns it, 'forty.'

The Dancing Room

That room.
I remember that room, where
the red darkness
gave itself up to green.
It was a square room.
No, it was a round room.
See how memory trips me up.
To think that I was ever there now.
To think that my legs contained that much light.
Now, they are strange shadowy horses.
I must pick them up to lead them at all,
as round the green field
they and I go.
They look at me as if they hardly know me.
'Has it come to this?' they ask.
'Can't you see the light that spills from the dancing room?
We can still see it. It is you who is blind.'
They are right.
I remember now. How it goes.
You open the door with your heart, and enter.
Right there where green light shifts
from under the door.
Where no shadows enter, save one.
The white light that comes from dancers –
have you never seen it?
I have bottled it in my mind's eye.
Brought it here for you.
This is how it goes.
It is a ripe fig on a green plate.
It is a monkey swinging its long legs from a silver tree.
It is a red gate that melts inside time, at your touch.
It is the underbelly, the shadow of dawn that walks abroad.
It is the need, and the dream, the being and the not-being
all in one.
It is the place that ends all beginnings.

How the light dazzles me.
It is cruel. It is wonderful.
Today, I am a ripe fig on a green plate.
I am cicada breath in the midnight, still.
I am the red fox who meets himself under the green moon.
Today, I am come back to the place I long for.
I can edge myself easily under the door.
The floor is the same, here nothing has changed.
The piano stands open – why did I wait?
My feet are cool roses. I remember this room.

My Red Sandals

My steps have no shadows.
My shoes are red.
It is a particular day.
My mother walks ahead of me.
Her steps make my way easy.
This is called holiday.
My feet have no shadows.
Nor are they strangers.
I am a child.
I am running to the beach in my red shoes.
The sand is made of diamonds and people's thoughts.
The clouds are made of ice-cream.
The sea is itself.
My shoes are good in rock pools.
My shoes are great over rocks.
My shoes are best on sand. This sand.
The sand is diamonds.
It fills my shoes with its thousand lives.

I can see what the sea thinks.
I want these shoes to last forever.
I want this moment to last always.
Not be swept away.

I am not afraid.

My blood is coral reef. My heart
a sudden pearl.
I am here now and I am here always.

I don't want the sea to swallow my red shoes
so I will leave my dears at the water's edge
where the water can talk to them. And now

I am looking back to the shore.
The sky is orange.
The day is lemon sherbet.
The sea is licking it.
I know everything the sea knows.
My shoes are two red boats
and in the deep of deeps alone I'm standing
and clear as clear my mother walks ahead of me.
My riding high, these waves, will last forever.

Nothing is any trouble.
Nothing is any trouble at all.

Inside my shoes, inside myself, diamonds.

Racing Caterpillars

Inch by inch, they emerge.
(We have a matchbox each.)
The path next to the cabbages is cold, grey.
And there's been rain. Good Yorkshire rain, which
hisses and steams in the yard like fighting cocks.
It talks about trouble at the mine and how money
may always be the other fellow's, and how
Dad's job is on the line, but –
we don't have ears that hear this yet.
We are racing caterpillars down by the Big Cut.
We've skived off school – where will that get us anyway?
Books and that.
Timing for each caterpillar is crucial.
But we get interruptions.
For now these are called parents and lessons.
Later they will be called marriage and kids.
But today, racing caterpillars, none of this matters.
We have new sandals on that Mam paid half a week's wages for.
Our feet were measured for them like a baby's corpse.
We have sherbet lucky dips lolling from our pockets.
We have used your maths test as the starting line.

Now we can see them. The runners emerge from the stands.
My caterpillar is too laid back.
It was a mistake to call him Ringo.
In defiance you have called yours Paul. But he is too cocky.
You are laughing so much that I know you'll be sick.
So I reckon,
I am in with a chance.
Just this once, eh?

The Gift

Today,
as if a gladness, a brightness
in the corner of my eye has gone.
As if a part of this timepiece, my heart,
were missing.
As if a face in the corner of my always room
were hidden.
As if a picture we had worked on –
your stitches, small and graceful –
were folded over, were held in another's arms
and for the moment, stored away.

Mother, a perfume steals over me
that is knotted with time.
It is both dark and light and is fretted like the sea.
The sea, the vast sea
so like the colour of your eyes.

Was it yesterday that we examined rings?
Three of them, silent in small blue boxes.
Three thin gold bands –
one with three white diamonds – 'like faces
shining in the night,' you said.

In the small room, I am sitting with you.
I am just sitting with you.
And we spoke of everything, as always and we
admired the rings, in the evening light,
the delicate, special rings.
Later, you close the boxes, one by one, and
as if in a dream, you hand them to me.
My hand over yours, I take them,
the pale room all around us
as if we are drowning, growing paler –
each wave rising higher than the last.
My hand over yours,
you give me treasure, one last time.

Bless This Handbag

At crucial moments of my life
you will find me ironing.
A trick learnt from my mother.
She always smoothed things out,
made peace between warring parties.
Now, the only creases left are around her eyes.

We meet in town, for coffee
and some sort of a cake.
She says she's taking sugar in tea again,
and perhaps I should.
I don't look well. Much too pale.

I manoeuvre the talk onto politics.
The Gulf, the Catholic viewpoint,
the new outlook on water births, legalising pot.
Undeflected, she overrides me with
a brief statement on
meringue and eggs you couldn't get in the war, then
back we go to my own queer pallor.

I wish I'd put more blusher on.
She toys with me like a footballer, playing me back and forth.
Or as if we're in a trench and she can constantly order me
over the top.
The confrontation is endless.
I wish I could learn this trick from her.
I wish I knew how the war could be won.
I wish I could eat meringue that fast.

I will my cheeks to glow with health as
she leads me across the No-Man's-Land of
combinations and corsetry, of
hosiery appliances and multi-size inner soles.
Everything the colour of a rich tea biscuit.

Playfully, she tweaks at a string vest as we pass.
'Call that a changing room? I wouldn't send a dog in there.'
Like a russet bomb, her handbag is ticking.
It is bright scarlet, goes with nothing that she wears.

Patiently, she shows me something that doubles as
an omelette scoop and a thing for killing wasps.
'If you're going to wear green for God's sake, do it on a Wednesday,'
she says,
and leaves it at that.
We narrowly miss a rail of pinnies.

Slowly we make our way to the bus stop.
Even this much walking is too much now.
I promise to eat more, but to smoke
and go out less.
She waits for the bus, handbag clutched stoically.

Inside it I can glimpse
two tins of rice pudding
and a bottle of Lourdes water – in case of emergency.
She climbs onto the bus. Hands me a separate package.
It's the third tin of rice pudding.

Even as the bus rounds the corner
I can still see the handbag, gathered to her,
its words of wisdom
like a million suns' rays, glinting, fabulous.
Eradicating all conflict, going over the top.

Avoiding Stories

Today I am avoiding stories, but everywhere I go things happen.
For instance, there is a new man come to clean the windows.
He says that my soul is in urgent need of a clean and that he –
as an emissary from God's honeycombed lair – can do it.
When I open the door to pay him, he is wearing only a bowler hat.
Nothing else.
I do not think he is from God, but just then I am called away to the
   phone.
It is you, to say you are being rushed to casualty as you have choked
on a piece of shoe leather which you mistook for beef and placed in
   a sandwich.
It was the piece I had put in the fridge to repair the lucky wind-
   chime someone
bought us, which fell on my foot mangling the top phalanx of my
   big toe.
I call a taxi to the hospital which, when it comes, is being driven
by the ex-monk I normally try to avoid. He has taken up taxi-ing as it
involves less shenanigans and fewer nuns.
(You can see how my avoidance has failed me, I think.)
We discuss how you can get cheap roof racks at Leeds-Bradford
   airport and how
in fact shoe leather can look like beef in a certain light.

When I get to casualty the receptionist makes me wait as long as
   she can as she
blames me for the fact that she can't retire for eight more years as
   her husband,
who was once in my job club, is still the lazy idle git he always was.
I am sent to the wrong cubicle where a vagrant is being treated for
   trapped wind.
Finally, I find YOU. You are now in the recovery position despite
   the fact
you have swallowed the best part of half a sandal.
WE EMBRACE.

A doctor comes in who, taking against my Irish surname, asks me if
it is normal Irish practice to leave shoe leather where innocent
   painter-and-decorators
might be tempted to eat it.
I explain I am not Irish, it's just the surname, but she will have
   none of it.
I think she would like a sample of my blood. All of it.
Eventually we manage to leave after a cup of tea from a trolley
   being driven by a man
called Bert who I remember from a watercolour class, as Barbara-
   Who-Likes-Shoes.
(I am reluctant to call another taxi, for fear of monks, so we decide
   to walk home.)
When we get there a group of about twenty gypsies have tethered
   two horses to our front gate
and are racing the third one chariot style down the street.

We sit on our wall and share an apple with the horses.

Sandra is a Child of Peace and Love

Sandra is five foot two.
Sandra is fierce, like Boadicea.
We are on our way to Knebworth
in an old jalopy,
my red hat is floppy and
I've got sandals on
and we've got joss sticks in the van.
Joni Mitchell is playing in the park
and we've borrowed Keith's van and we're off to
Knebworth for a lark.

Sandra works at Woolies –
plastic roses, care of Daz, decorate her hair.
If you can remember Sandra in the Sixties
you probably weren't there.
Me – I'm a rebel in my leopard-skin pill-box hat
and Sandra – she's a child of peace and love.

I've been selling Oz magazine in the High Street again,
I'm a student, I'm a rebel, when they call at my door –
me mam's packed me sandwiches, I said I'll be home by four.
I've got a dahlia in my hair –
if you can remember me and Sandra
you just *so* were not there –
me I'm a rebel, quintessential psychedelic,
and Sandra, she's a child of peace and love.

It's 1994, when I meet Sandra again –
she says: 'What you doing now pet?
Do you fancy a cup of tea,
we can nip down to Greggs, I've got the 40p.
Barry? The one with the headband,
he's living in Oz now –

I wish I'd never met him, what a flaming square –
as far as happiness goes, he was definitely not there.
Do you remember I was a child of peace and love?'

She says all the bairns have gone
and she's divorced twice now –
she's doing a course in self-development – worra laugh –
about bloody time eh?
There are lines around her eyes,
which is no surprise to me, no not at all.
When we pass the flower seller in the Big Market,
I can almost smell that perfume of when we didn't have a care.
She says: 'Do you remember?'
I say – of course not – we were there.
I'll always be a rebel. And you are still a child of peace and love.

Why I Fancy Him

It's something to do with the way
his shoulders grip life
as he walks down the road to the match.
Like a warrior into battle.
Something to do with the scent of his dreams
on the pillow next to mine.
Something about the way he can't choose
holiday shorts without me. Something about the way he stands
while poaching us both an egg and
reading the match results.
Something about the fact that the answer phone buttons baffle him.
Something about the way he still manages a smile
as he picks up the forty-fifth shell from the beach,
that JUST might be the one.
Something about his look over the top of the newspaper
when I mention (again) this amazingly cheap trip
to Portuguese monasteries or how you can track down the
Lost Orchid of the Incas and stay with a genuine relative
of Montezuma – if you book early enough.
Something about his dazzling display of monkey walks
that gets us thrown out of an art gallery.
Something about the way he ties up flowers in the garden
trying to make the process both invisible and painless.
Something about the way he gets entangled in his own cagoule.
Something about the way he balances casually on top of a forty-foot
    ladder,
and shouts down he'll have a ninety-nine in his cornet,
but no raspberry sauce.
Something about the way he falls asleep reciting a love-poem
and cradling a half-eaten banana.
Just, something.

The Ruby Slippers

You come in to the shop with me and
we take my new false leg off and
look around for an assistant but
they all seem to be very busy breathing and
polishing the shoes in the window.
Which is strange because they don't look the polishing type.
I have seen the pair I want.
They are red and exotic of course and
I would like to point to them but
a small elderly man comes out from the back-room
(where I think he has been in storage since 1940)
makes eye-contact with you and asks you what you would like.

You say you would like to be treated like a normal human being.
All the assistants stop polishing now, to listen.
Which is strange because they don't look the listening type.
The man says he fought in a war for people like us
and where has it got him?
Then he accidentally knocks my wheelchair and has to make eye-
    contact
with me which is painful to him. Just like the war was.
Then, he wheels me to where they keep
the selection of trainers that nobody buys, and walks off back to
    1940.

We were happy before we came in.
We had bought chocolates and Parma ham and
we were oh so happy.
Now, you are frothing at the mouth and I have fixed that smile on
    my face
like Harry Corbett, when he used to say –
'Bye bye, everybody, bye bye.'
when Sooty had done something wrong and he was covered in flour
    and water.

Then, as if by magic – the ruby shoes get up and walk out of the window
and climb up onto my knee and apologise.

And all the assistants suddenly want to open doors for us and bow and scrape and help us get the hell out.
Which is strange because they don't look the opening doors type.
So, we leave, with those ruby slippers clinging on to us for dear life and
I want to say: 'Don't you know – I'm fighting in a war for people like you.'

But, I don't. And Kansas? It just gets further and further away.

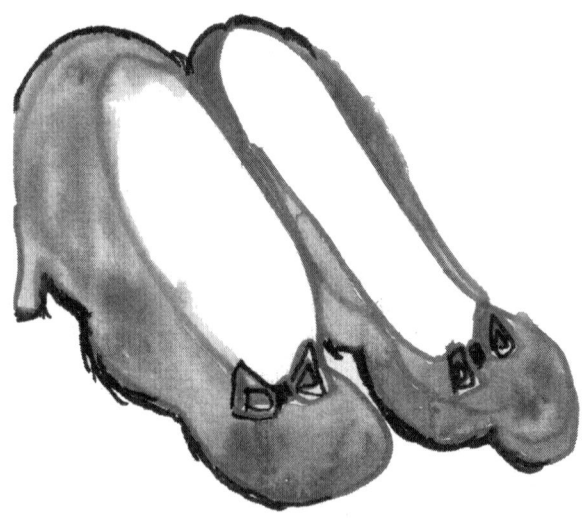

The Green Field

I dreamed I was a horse
and the green field all around me
kissed my feet.
In my eyes two doves smiled
and the sun and moon were mine
in equal measure.
The day was music within my bones.
The night was music within my blood
and I was blessed.

And blessed
I ran within that green field, where,
in its sweetest, farthest corner I saw
lay buried a silver-box – so small,
yet within the box,
lay the root, the tree,
the waiting forest of my dreams.

And from this, I ran.
And ran, and ran, far, far from it, until –
at last, I saw it no more –
and was sad.
For years I ran and ran and ran – until –
the moon it was that stopped me. Under her light,
I looked down and saw that
within my own body lay that green field,
within my own heart lay that silver box.
Still and silent – in the moon's light.

Waiting.

Owls

Tonight,
the moon is a river.
A silver shadow whose face we admire.
The moon turns the river's pages
like a book.
Softly, the pages turn, one by one.
In the river ourselves, our faces, turning.
Here, where the edges of trees frisk our shadows
and trace the night shapes of houses –
we are watching for owls.
I am convinced they are near.

It is only that the dark trees are hiding them.
It is only that the old boats are hiding them.
The owls fly inside my own eyes – in and in,
flying lower and lower. My thoughts become feathers.
My dreams have no edges. Flight swallows me.
I am owl and moon and river and night.
The stars watch over me – the pulse of the water
greets me, keens for me
that I must watch here, so late. It is the hour for owls.
I hear the slow beating of their coming.
A train passes, holds the moon in each of its windows.
Myself, I am held by the promise of owls.
My throat holds a shadow, it grows and grows
and from it
flies the first of them.

At the Foreigners' Club

At first, at the Foreigners' Club
we wear our English-ness with pride.
It is expected of us.
We say: 'Bring us your finest marmalade –
but not your Marmite, for we have brought our own
in small tartan shoppers bought in Epping.'
We ask how the eggs are fried and if
the man who batters the fish
comes from a real family of batterers. (If not, we send it back.)

In the huge Venetian mirrors, the waiters
move serenely like tall ships
moving in and out of difficult harbours.
They all sing – though one whistles – 'Figgy Pudding.'

There is a strange English-ness about him.
The other waiters hoot and toot and call out:
'Mamma Mia – we are having you replaced Figgy Pudding.
There is always tomorrow to be English –
be English when you are dead.
Right now we are bringing you Neapolitan ice-cream
made by our own grandmothers.'

We hitch up our baggy shorts and leave the bar inside
(with its pots of tea and trifle) empty.
We drift outside to a boulevard of pistachio and a peach sunrise.
We lie on the grass like emperors – our
skin speckled with icing sugar, rose petals and violets. (What devils
  we are.)

For a little while we watch the vanilla sunset.
For a little while, we are Italian.

On the 14th Deck of the Cruise Ship Aurora

No one wears beige on the fourteenth deck.
No one wears sailor suits and plays deck quoits.
No one invites us to a chocoholics buffet or
asks thirty Indian chefs to limbo-dance
through a gateaux of mousse-lined Viking ships.
There is a strange light from this Captain's eyes.
This floor is made of Cape daises and kept promises.
The portholes glisten with honeysuckle and ragged robin.
The Captain wears nothing and he advises we do the same.
Things are different here.
Our bodies become young again and softly entwined in each other.
The flowers become entwined in our bodies, until
between flesh and flowers there is no difference.
Here, the moon keeps time in its small hand and the sun plays a
  mandolin.
It is a medley of voices we had thought lost forever.
There is a river we may bathe in and become free again.
Our hearts are happy as drooping fuchsias that nod in time
to the road that leads to the sea.
Our foxglove fingers and forget-me-not souls will not be parted.
We break and bend in the wind from the ocean as if we were one
  person.
Our old skin uncurls from the body like an onion-ring
and our new self uncurls and touches the stars.
On the fourteenth deck, all is known – and no one is a stranger.
Even those who never met, remember where it was.
The Captain has a bugle in the shape of a moose with huge crystal
  antlers.
This moose calls down the sky and calls up the sea
and where the two meet – a young deer and a lion walk.
The Captain is measuring the clouds and the deer and the lion walk
  together freely.
All problems disappear here.

There is no yesterday or tomorrow on the fourteenth deck,
there is only NOW –
lovely, glorious, carefree hope-filled NOW.

Push the button in the lift, my love, and take me there.

The Rehabilitation Hobbies Room

This is recuperation then, this is rehabilitation.
Here by learning how to re-tie my own anxiety into bows
I will be made whole again.
From all the hobbies on the hobby table
I shall choose sand. Sand and ribbon-reading.
By my ribbons they will know me.
I send back the mirrors made from pasta twirls.
I send back the soft toy dogs made from
cotton wool and silly tape.
The gnomes and plaster cast of Jesus (the champagne
corks still wobbling) I eschew.
These are the glories of the hobby room
where we must come before they sign us out, we damaged moths.

I must sketch my own silhouette in beer can tops and
draw my own eyes with sea-foam and silicone.
I must re-join my bones with cement and sloe-gin.
I must position my mended shadow on the wall of reason.
I must play football with my own spleen,
badminton with my own kidney.
I must leave a sample of my own cheerfulness in the cup provided.
I must fashion a prophecy from eggshells and straw.
My hobby is leaving – this is my choice.
I will not choose another.
My lilac wings are beating a pattern in the clear space above my head.

Stay in Touch

'You will, won't you – you WILL stay in touch,' she said.
'Of course,' we said – well,
that's to say, we tried.
Wrote letters, sent photos, even once a present.
(What a couple of fools.)
But it seemed life was busier for her than us.
So we never heard squat.
Then ten years later, she saw us in the town, and wept.
'I would have stayed in touch, but, it's just not my forte –
things got on top of me,
the years and jobs and men.
But, NOW, the kids have gone
(moved to the moon to be nearer their dad).
Now I've nothing else doing and I'm miserable as sin
and I'm throwing a breakdown party this very Saturday,
now my life no longer fits or suits me.
You both MUST come. I simply won't take no for an answer.

Yes – this time – I really WILL stay in touch.'

Drawing Dogs

I have taken to drawing dogs.
They have begun to seem more like people than people.
I feel more certain that they will
inherit the Earth.
I feel safer when a dog snarls
than when a person smiles.
I can see them deciding not to think of all the answers
before they've eaten their dinner.
I can see they're not bothered if the post is late or if
they miss the bus to Fulham Broadway.
Their faces do not pose when you look at them
(and then try to pretend that they've just seen you).
If they're happy, they're happy – and sad if they're sad.
If they got begging letters – they would answer all of them.
In their heads, all of them are riding motorbikes across France
without a care in the world.
And most brilliantly of all – they do not write poetry.
I like dogs.

The Shape of Hands

Mother,
your bright shadow with me all the day.
Like a distant butterfly. All the day.
Hidden by the sun.

Unable to catch sight of your flight,
I look at the space you have left.
I am just too slow, too intent and though
I look and look,
I miss where you fly, how your wings are unclaimed
by the heaviness of day.
Above me, all around me, your shadow sings a new song.

On the wall, the shadow of my own hand
as night falls.
I look and see it is
the exact shape of yours,
even the way it holds the light against
the outstretched glove of darkness. Incredible how
the cupped shape is the same.

Darkness falls, and though I cannot see the lines
that court this shadow palm, borrowed from you –
I know your flight still follows me.
Together we will see the journey out,
trace our shapes against a different sky, but for now
we have spent the day together, after all.

Tomorrow

Tomorrow, there will be enough
of food, and warmth and love, and hope.

Tomorrow, the birds WILL sing.

Tomorrow, fear and hate will be outlawed
and dreams, good dreams, will have a place
in everybody's lives.

Tomorrow, the birds WILL sing.

Tomorrow, there will be no more calls to arms,
to war.
No more pitting soul against soul
until even the bravest dies a little inside.

Tomorrow, the birds WILL sing.

Tomorrow, you will see there is
a reason to go on,
a light that shines,
a field that beckons –
in truth, there will be all you ever hoped for.
You will walk in peace
in the green field, under the sun
that warms, that mends.

Until then, take heart, friend
and be glad you live.
Touch each life you meet
with your own truth
and with this just and certain hope –

Tomorrow, the birds WILL sing.
For each, for everyone.

The Road Out of Town

When will I take you, I ask –
the road out?
Will it be tomorrow? Will it?

Oh, let it be tomorrow –
sweet as a peach that road
and you, juicy with laughter.
Rich that road, as rich as rich
with peacock beginnings
and myself with the shackles and the blindfold gone
and this other road – forgotten.
At first we will be dizzy with the joy of it
but that won't matter – no –
just the feel of the road under our feet
shaking the dust of ages,
the cruel hands of time from ourselves.
Just the being gone will be enough.

No barriers. No signposts.
Just the sun shining on new black tar.
The smell of it under our feet.
And my little famine bones, mending again.
With each bold step as further out of town
I with my singing heart and my whistling soul am led.

And you will look around – oh yes
and only know that I am gone.
You will see the space I have left and say:
'Why yes – there was somewhere else she had to be,
a path she always had to tread'.

And you will hear me singing still
as all sing when first they take that single step
on the Road out of Town.

— from *And God Said Let There Be Chocolate* (2013) —

And God Said Let There Be Chocolate

And there was.
Lashings of it. Whole mountain ranges of it.
Dark and white, filled with rum and raisin –
landscapes of nougat covered in it,
streets awash with it –
men on street corners peddling it,
people stood on soap boxes warning about the end of the world
and how we should all make provision. Lay in stores of it.
Cradles of it – bamboozles of it, yards of it like freshly ironed calico
coming right off conveyor belts and into the mouth.
Leaving God in no doubt that the angels had been here.
Gabriel at his finest, best.
Making little caramel cookies filled with chocolate wedges,
dreams of chocolate – white lakes of it with chocolate cherry
 paddles that
take you upstream to where the cocoa monster lives.
Am I telling it like it is?
Special moments in life – filled with a chocolate kinda haze –
happiness is chocolate shaped.
Banana flavoured, cracknel glazed – such wickedness exists.
You love it – the light of it, the break of it, the unrelenting crunch
 of it
The spring bird melting way of it.
And on the Eighth Day. God saw what he had done.
Knew it would be tough.
And so. He relented. And made.
Chocolate.

Chocolate Credo

I believe in chocolate.
I believe that chocolate is a gift from the Gods and
should be used accordingly.
I believe in hundreds and thousands being sprinkled on it
and bars of it being eaten all of a piece. No messing.
I believe that chocolate is the giver of life and a happy soul.
I believe that chocolate is what they made Christmas for and that
chocolate bunnies had it coming to them.
I believe in chocolate.
And that it preceded human beings is obvious.
There has always been chocolate since cave man times.
Chocolate was brought here by another race called the Deliciosas.
They were small and friendly and had chocolate buttons on their
  coats
and saw how Earth was struggling and so
they gave us chocolate.
They left a large cocoa pod for early man to find outside the cave
one Christmas morning and we have never looked back.
I believe in the Deliciosas and all they stood for.
They knew we just might make it through if we had chocolate to
  fall back on.
Whole mountains of it; whole babbling brooks of it; whole
  fountains of it.
I believe in the truth of the crispy caramel bar and the hope hereafter
of always having a tube of Smarties or a Dime bar somewhere in
  easy reach.
I believe that there is a good tomorrow for you and me, as long as
we clap our hands – all together – and
continue to believe in chocolate.
The Holy Grail of it – the Swinging my legs on a Gate of It –
the Deliciosa legacy of CHOCOLATE!

The Refuseniks

These folk are refugees from the Land of Chocolate.
They refuse it. They turn it down, as if it were lethal.
No, no they say – our figures… tch tch, we must think again.
They see it in the shop and avert their gaze and buy
sugar-free chewing gum and a magazine about a woman who
can now fit in a matchbox. Her husband is proud, we all are.
When did the rot set in?
As children or as grown women?

Do they remember running out for ice creams, the 99s
in the middle, left to the last? That perfect crunch.
Or the little chocolate sprinkles on the birthday cakes?
They sit at the far end of the tea room, with their lettuce sandwiches
on rye – and special yoghurt. Gazing out through the window
and across the whole of Birmingham.
Her husband's in the pub, fourteen
floors down – with the blonde lass from accounts whose flesh
he can grip in handfuls. (The less there is of his wife – the more
she'll get promoted.) She is the thinnest of the refuseniks that I know.
You get a broom out of the staff room, and we all see the likeness
to Cherry.

The Little Chocolate Soldier

He knew his place in the toy room.
He knew he wasn't REAL like them, his guns
were made of candy and his hat was vermicelli.
He knew he was looked down upon because he could not fight.
He knew he'd never go to war.
That dividing line Big Ted had drawn across the toy room floor.
What did it mean? And why?
What had the clockwork robot done to Ted to cause him this much
   grief?
And if he spoke out what then? Would they snap him in two?
His chocolate heart ached, but he knew the score.
So, he watched all of life from a very high window
and in his own way, waged a quite different war.

In Which Dad is 'Dances With Chocolate'

Like some old Injun – that was me dad.
On a Friday night, him and me, watching the late film –
maybe a good Bette Davis or Casablanca –
all being well
and there would always be chocolate.
But ONLY Fry's cream. Or a good bar of Terry's dark.
None of your lightweight stuff.
Not on a Friday night. Not watching Bogart.
And in the drawer in the kitchen – bags of chocolate waste
that friends had brought. There for small emergencies
and little known saints' days.
But for *Casablanca* and *Inn of the Sixth Happiness*
and – (if we were lucky) – *The Maltese Falcon* –
only Terry's dark would do.
And dad would dance while he watched. Glad of the end
of the working week – and the club tomorrow night
(a few pints). And chocolate was the totem of our tribe.
And we two would smoke the pipe of peace from all our arguing.
And watch Bergman catch that plane into the night.
And mam would be Stands And Says Do You Want A Cup Of Tea
   or What?
And I would be Writes It All Down With Hope in The Heart.
This was and is my tribe. And no need for cavalry coming over the
   hill.
Only the great unvanquished spirit of the earth.
Only the wise words that make smoke rings in the heart.
(And Terry's dark.)

The Creature from the Chocolate Lagoon

Always on a Friday it happened –
before they clocked off. Like it knew
it was home time, have a brew time, finish
early time.
The creature.
Along the conveyor belt and into the whirlpool of
chocolate it dived. It looked like a bird, no,
maybe a giraffe – or partly a lizard.
Brenda said, all lizard, from where she was standing.
But Barry said, no, not a lizard from where, at the top
of the stairs he was stood. More like an anteater, with
the tail of a bushbaby and the haunted eyes of
a cat, with eight lives used up. And Archie ran at it
and grappled it down, and they thought – ha! – at last we've got you.
But no way, Jose.
The creature was smart as an alley cat's dad – as a slippery
eel, as a box of delicious after dinner whatsits.
And it squeezed right out of young Archie's grasp and ran
pell-mell and coated itself in the nougat and coated
itself like some weird sugared ghost.
The shape of the head, why
it almost had antlers, and the feet were the best –
all six of them made of pure marzipan – and the blue
of its nose, well it fair made you shudder.
But Angela – new to the finishing room – was the one
who managed to calm it, managed to talk it down and
turn things around. She knew its language (how, we don't know).
She lived in Tang Hall and spoke Esperanto and was
learning Italian at night class in Burnholme, so the creature
seemed calmer, knew that it could trust her.
She took it home on the number ten bus.
Her mam, a kind soul, fed it fish fingers, baked beans.
And so, it is that the Creature from the Chocolate Lagoon
still lives there.

And, as Angela says, such creatures are rare.
And the friendship it craved was all that it wanted.
Just for someone to speak kindly and show that they care.
It waves her off, and packs up her lunch box –
and is trying real hard, with Italian.

The Smarties Room

Even in chocolate, there is a hierarchy.
The red smarties do not like the yellow
and the yellow have got it in for the purple ones.
The orange smarties say they make no apology
for being the best. The green smarties are in denial
and no one wants the blue ones – they can
cook their goose elsewhere. Who thought them up?
There is to be an inquiry in the Kit Kat room.
There is a revolution planned where the Lion Bar
makes its way down to the sea.
There is talk of a new bar – one that we have waited for,
one that will bring peace and hope and calm to all.
Some say it has been here before, but we dismissed it
as before its time.
John tells me the cocoa mix must be refined a few
thousand times – and then stirred by beautiful maidens.
He came to us, was head-hunted, from Bournville,
so no one is too sure of what he means.
He wants to call the bar – the Promise.
He eats, sleeps and dreams chocolate.
There is a competition in the canteen to name the bar,
Hug-It, Snaffle and RumbleTums almost have it.
But, in the end, Christine from Packing is inspired –
let's call it Yummy-Yummy, she says.
And the rest is history.
(Even in the Smarties room – peace is declared.)

The Chocolate Angel

Mam believed in angels.
Whole hordes of them – guardian angels, saints' day angels,
angels that kept you out of mischief. Angels that helped
you do your homework, even maths. But –
is there a chocolate angel, I asked. One that means that
if the end of the world should come even before
Sister Angela says it will – which is because she is being sent back to
Dublin by the way, and as English heathens we are for it –
Maureen McDonald had probably felt the benefit in later life of
spending the weekend tied to a chair with five pairs of rosary
beads… would she not…
What if someone stole all the chocolate in the world and held
us all to ransom? What if???
But mam believed in angels. Angels would sort things out –
would see me through the tough times, the not so great times.
And she would know the reason why… or else.
But for now – just for now – yes, we could stop at the little
shop on the corner and admire Ted's garden
and get a stick of licorice and a pink sugar mouse.
And the chocolate angel?
Sure – that will be your dad. Hard at work at Rowntree's.
And he'll be home later.
And at the end of the week – depending how things go –
there might be chocolate in a bag.
Something special, something precious. Something to aim for.
Until then,
aay your prayers and do your sums.
And avoid Sister Angela.

Dad and Terry's Factory

Dad was three minutes late at the factory gate.
So, that was that.
Ended up working for the M.O.D.
which he wasn't cut out for – anyone could see.
But three minutes late – and that was that.
Aunt Sarah begged and Aunt Lella cried
but the woman in the Office, she said
my hands are tied.
So, that was that.
The fact he'd been knocked off his bike?
What did that matter.
Compensation? What the hell's that.
A poor young Irish lad – fell to earth with a clatter.
Aunt Sarah cried and Aunt Lella begged –
got down on her hands and knees at the factory gate –
but 200 more stood in line for his job. And one of them got it.
So, that was that. The end of the line, the chance in a million.
The luck of the Irish is not always lucky.
Not in dad's case as he frequently told me.
Ended up digging gas pipes and laying more down – out
in all weathers. Ain't so good for your health.
Ended up mending boilers – riding his bike
through blizzards at four in the morning. Just
to pay the rent, keep food on the table.
The working class – let's make them old before their time.
Three minutes late at the factory gate.
Sometimes, in life, that's all it takes.
A chance in a million. The end of the line.

Uncle Pa's Drawer

Uncle's drawer was full of it – chocolate of every size
and shape. Toffees, eclairs, bars of white chocolate and
bars of dark chocolate.
Mary Anne toffees and Caramac bars nestled against
starched white handkerchiefs, table cloths, a small wooden
camel all the way from Damascus, a medal from the Boer War.
I was led to the drawer on special occasions – Easter Sunday,
Pa's birthday, my birthday – and a gem would be retrieved.
Handed to my small outstretched hand.
Pa seemed so tall – like some fairy godfather of chocolate.
The day seemed to glow with chocolate – the world a wild
honeycomb awaiting my touch. (Six years old and all to play for.)

All these years later – with you, in Wilkinson's – I look for the
 Caramac bar.
And remember Uncle Pa. And those gifts of chocolate.
And the world is mine again.
Briefly, mine.

The Empress of Chocolate

I am the Empress of Chocolate – and
on the Street of Good Fortune in Pompeii
is my home. Chocolate is my favourite subject.
There are no rules for him. He can come and go
as he chooses.
My father lives on the Street of Miracles – and is
ruler of the Holy Roman Empire.
They carry me in a sedan chair to the theatre.
My name is Livia. Bring me chocolate
and worship at my shrine. All of Rome loves me,
don't they? In my ears I hear the people cheering
as they see me.
I am a fair Empress, and a good Empress.
As long as you remember to worship me with chocolate.

Les Petits Chiens de Paris

are everywhere.
They adorn the ladies' arms, they trot behind
the men buying baguettes.
They travel in small baskets across the Bois de Boulogne.
They look as snug as a bug in a chocolat rug.
Life is fantastique – life is unique – they bark.
Some live on the Left Bank and some live on the Right –
Les petits chiens de Paris.
They dip their feet in the fountains at the Louvre,
they lie spreadeagled against the sun dials at the Tuileries –
exquisite. Enjoying a hearty picnic.
They pose for paintings that their owners will adore
and compare to the blue dancers of Degas.
They bark at fleas at flea markets, they know why
the Mona Lisa smiles. Les petits chiens de Paris –
they travel in Vuitton handbags, in le sac next to le Blackberry,
In their one paw, fromage; in the other a glass of wine.
None of them speaks English and all of them – très beau.
They are all so chic – they nibble doggie chocolates
at midnight. The sun shines in all their eyes. Exquisite.

The Chocolate Bird in the Garden

Tells me that today, it is spring.
Chocolate is springing up everywhere – chocolate blossom
is hanging from the trees and bulbs of chocolate
are pushing through the soil.
Everyone is out in their gardens, tending their nougat bushes
and watering the marzipan floribunda.
My dad is weeding the dark chocolate path that leads to the gate
and mam is watching him – sat drinking cocoa
and planning a fudge cake for tea for him and me.
Spring goes with chocolate and chocolate goes with spring.
Both are a time of new beginnings – little vermicelli birds
fly over and dogs bury chocolate bones where only they can
find them. And I can see how beautiful the world is.
As I sip the sunshine of the day.
May your day and your life go well.
I wish you spring. I wish you chocolate.

— from *Here's Looking at You, Kid* (2014) —

Here's Looking at You, Kid

I noticed from an early age that the sun
asked permission to be on our street.
'Is the sun allowed here?' I once asked me dad,
and even though he knew it wasn't
he pulled his collar high and looked all round –
then put it in his pocket just for me.
Even though he knew to own this bright,
this dangerous thing would bring me
perils, as well as joy.
(Better to have a little sun than none at all.)

And we walked home, like two happy dogs
and the sky was duck-egg blue and the grass
was full of four-leaved clovers
and dad winked – and we laughed to think
he had the sun in his pocket.

'Here's looking at you, kid,' dad said.
'Here's looking at you.'

Dad's Lingo

You ask me what his lingo was
and the only way I can explain is this:
the Irish for yes – is no
and the Irish for no – is yes.
If he said he liked someone, that meant that he only *tolerably*
hated them.
If he said he couldn't stand them
at any price nor be in the same room even –
this meant he had definitely warmed to them,
would be prepared to have a drink with them. Give them the benefit
of some soldierly, hard won advice. Oh, yes.
If he said he would do a thing directly – this meant you could wave
it bye bye.
Permanento.
As much chance as a female pope. As likely as him selling his Mario
Lanza LPs.
If he said he could not, *would* not be persuaded, no, not even if a
glass of Guinness
stood between the thing and himself – you could guarantee success
within the hour.
Sooner, quicker than a gnat's dream. As certain as a plenary
indulgence.
This was my father's lingo.
And to say I understood it – does not do him justice. Part of the
time I understood part of him
and all of the time I understood none of him – although *some* of
the time he allowed me
to think that I had followed the circuitous path of his extraordinary
thinking. Oh, yes.
And the rest of the time – he translated what he could. Myself, the
poor eejut.
He allowed me to believe that I had made sense of his words.
But behind my back – I knew he was laughing. (And I am so glad
he was.)
The Irish for yes – is no
and the Irish for no – is yes.

The Kids with the Tree House

How we hated them.
Then. The unthinkable – they asked us to tea.
Me and our lad.
So, we went.
Trudged up to the Big House, walked on the gravel
(what the hell's that?) Mummy showed us the way.
The garden – jeez – the size of the park
and them sitting up in their lofty domain.
You watched as they climbed the ladder, high into the leafy
green world. All luscious and beckoning.
We followed. Drank from the acorn cups,
ate off the bamboo plates. Little May had brought Teddy up.
You held him to ransom, by his leg right over the edge.
You kicked the ladder away as we scrambled off.
The boy tried to be brave, but May screamed and screamed.
They were no match for you – with their acorn agenda and gravel
stupendous. We ran, all the way home.
And you had egg and chips, and went out with the bad lads
from the dodgy end of the street.
And I couldn't eat mine – kept seeing May's face.
And mam said – 'How was it? Tea with the posh lot?'
And I said – 'Can we have a tree house?'
And mam said – 'There's the park down the road. How many
trees do you bloody want?'

Hospital Lingo

There's a lot of it about
in here.
It starts with 'the procedure', which will be
carried out whether I like it or not. Makes no odds – you can be
watching *Deal or No Deal* – and they'll still do it.
It will be done with a bicycle pump and a packet of Caramac.
Then a pair of tweezers – and I'll be smeared all over with
a sausage roll. It's for me own good.

Chrissie at the end is having everything removed,
piece by piece – her sanity, her sense of humour, her husband.
She's quite glad about the last.
Another poor sod is having all her bits sewn back *on,* but this time
in the right order. (The spleen is such an undecorative item.)
And the bag it came in – hers to keep, if she wants. There's thoughtful.
We have all been here longer than we would like.
Our visitors – poor limping specimens – come in just to cheer
themselves up. They are free to leave – cocky beggars.
We compare.
I've had mine scraped and flagellated and crimped. Then run up a
  flag pole. And still
it works with all the good grace of a banjo with no strings.
Maureen has had a pipe put down and a frog inserted where the
  blue dye spilled out. The frog is none too happy, either.
Cynthia – bless – has had it all twirled around and blown up, so all
  the first year students could get
a really good look – then she was rinsed and parboiled and a
hollandaise mouse was frozen in a time capsule and buried in her
second-best handbag. (Like on Masterchef.)
The woman who used to be a vicar – has been Emanuelled and
had the tattoo of Cliff Richards finally removed. She had a vision in
  the night of Bjorn from Abba giving her the kiss of life. Which is
  a worry.
And the little lass in the side room (sectioned) keeps *on* singing –
'we'll meet again Kathleen' – then running naked down to the front
  doors. Why wouldn't she – she's been Nil By Life since she was
  born.
Anyway – it's an ill wind – because –
they come in later to tell me that it's all going on nicely.
Just the inner tube to remove in the morning from me arse,
and the orang-utan to strap to me chest, and the whistling giraffe to
  come up with me tablets, and I can go.
Still, they do a lovely bit of fish – on a Friday.
If only it were Friday.
Is it Friday?
Is it?

French Cat in French Window

So. I am a French cat in a French window and you
are just passing by – you take my photograph –
why wouldn't you? – because I am beautiful.
I am beautiful – and you are English – that's how the cookie
    crumbles – yes, life can be unfair. Life can be a dog.
I am licking my arse – and I am still beautiful – don't try
it yourself. I can't be responsible for hospital bills.
I am a French cat in a French window – you are on your
way to – how you say it – Yorkshire?
I am on my way to Montmartre to buy a little sardine
on a bed of couscous – perhaps a little wine, if the year
she seems a good one. You look very pale – as if
your whole world, she is not coloured in and has no
way of turning the other cheek – and looking up at the moon
and singing in the night. At midnight.
That is when the French cat comes to life.
I myself run a little café in the Bois de Boulogne. I even
let a few English sit at the tables there. But, at this moment
I am cleaning my bottom – with the care of an artiste –
and you take my photograph.
I feel a little sorry for you – but even so, as you click your camera
I will turn my arse right around to face you.
This is – how you call it? –
the French Resistance.

The Serving Girl

Though I never knew her
I bear her name.
Margareta. My grandmother.
She is undismissable.
Sitting at the sea's edge,
a moon-faced dog at her side.
Eyes – neat as jet.
Skin the colour of turtledoves.
The lick of salt in her hair,
dark with time.

Here, next to her, is a blue pot that mutters.
Let us call it, the sea.
It contains all the words we never spoke.
It is held in our four hands
that never touched.
Fierce as flint, the years that lie between us.
Plaiting and unplaiting the dark memory
of your hair.
Though I never knew you, I bear your name.

I imagine the stairs you climbed in the grand house.
The starched minute hand of the clock
ticking in the hall.
The mistress of the house checking your apron.
Your presence in your own absence.
Nothing to be done but bear it.
I imagine the meals on silver trays carried back and forth.
The perfectly folded white cloths.
All with initials. None of them yours.
I can almost smell the blooms of white clematis
as it hung near your window.
In winter they will cut it back, and you will miss it so.

Did the house have a hundred rooms? I want to ask.
And was yours the finest Margareta?
Your secret name that lies on cloth invisible,
that now must serve for memory.
Only her voice, that is the salt, that is the sea,
answers me.

I swill her voice around my empty head.
I watch the tide that cannot call her home.
A prism of water in my throat. My throat that
glinting, swells, becomes the sea.
A final call that earths two names. A shaft of sunlight.
Our meeting now – like this. Incredible.
The pure chance of her wave ending
right where mine began.

The Old Pig

He was old, you told me.
The pig I now imagine, hanging sweet as a bag of sugar out in the barn.
Your job was always to feed him – and him
licking your hand as if it were pressed silk.
So many times, you told me the story.
Your guts turning, churning – knowing his future.
Brushing the long crease of your skirt –
watching him eat. Fat, contented.
Turning the iron handle of the sty door –
a kind jailor you must have seemed.
The sky above the door – blue as your eyes.
And the straw in his heart – stiff with fright on that last day.
Both of you willing that day not to come, but knowing it would.
Your face turned away to the sky –
love and anguish mixed with mud – a bloody cocktail.
Every ambush requires that there are two.
Your hand on the door, closing it.
The old pig, listening for your voice, found only silence.
Turn his face to the sky you tell the men.
You replay the ambush many times through all the years.
Because the pig forgives you.
Endlessly.
Even as they bring the knife towards him.
He forgives you.

The Kindness Medal

This is a medal for kind people.
It was minted in the
Can't-Be-Arsed-To-Be-Bothered-With-Them factory.
It will be ignored, not even brought out
on special occasions, like days that you breathe on, and
it will be stored in vaults, and knocked-down shacks
and will-o'-the-wisp caves and dust-riddled libraries that
no one, not even Philip Larkin, ever go in –
and it will be unsung about and unwritten about
and spiders will weave webs around it and its colour
will fade and the ribbon it would have hung from
will be lost and the little gold box it came in
will be broken and stood on and splintered
and no one will know, or worse, care.
It will be unremembered in a thousand small ways
in every city in the glib and transient world.
This is the Medal of Honour, for Kind People
and it will never, ever, be given to them.

My Wild Mother

My mother's at that difficult age
between 81 and 81-and-a-half.
She says she's not a senior citizen,
just a citizen.
She plays hooky from church bazaars,
borrows my kitten mules and feather boa
and hangs round bars in town.
Wears gold studs through her false teeth.
Has had a Lancaster bomber
tattooed on her left arm.
(We won't talk about her right.)
Men from the over-sixties club
leave things for her in the porch
in plain brown wrappers.

She says she's saving chat-rooms
for the New Year. After Bruges.
When she's bored.
Did I mention Bruges?
There's been talk of Bruges for Christmas
with Hal, the American she met
at salsa class. (Sixty-four, all his own teeth.)
She's fitting him in between life-modelling for
the man who mends the boiler
and shamanic journeying to rid herself
of life's little obstacles.
(Me, apparently.)

She buys shop cakes recklessly, now she no longer bakes.
My father's allotment has become a figure of fun and she
was seen giving the last of its produce to the poor and needy
at the DSS. (That's the staff.)
I can't bring myself to ask why it has to be a lift
at the Co-op to scatter dad's ashes.
She has been banned from the Countrywomen's Guild
for rap-dancing and spitting.
Her talk on Voodoo – 'How it can improve your sex life' –
has been put on indefinite hold.

Everyone says there's no need to worry.
That they're all the same at that age. It's just their hormones
    running amok.
That it's just a phase we'll look back on and laugh.
The sign on her bedroom door still reads – 'Access denied
to those not from the Planet Zog.'
Apparently – if I want to keep her –
I'll have to let her go.
(It's all very complicated.)
All I know is – her Perry Como collection lies in pieces in the bin
and underneath her pillow, there's a one-way ticket. (Bruges).

The Christmas Letter

Hallo.
This is just to let you know that
we're doing an awful lot
better than you.
Jessica got her PhD in
terminal snobbery
and Joshua hopes not to work, too.
We've got mummy with us
still in the annexe –
you'd hardly know she was there,
except for the odd fallout of money
and last few bits of hair.

We've had ten holidays, all of them foreign,
and Jem's wedding at the Abbey was fab.
The Caribbean beckons for Christmas, again,
and my new facelift's arrived from the lab.
Life is going swimmingly. And we do –
swim, that is, whenever we can.
We've been walking in Tuscany, the Dordogne and Sidcup,
and we're friends of a friend of Cherie's old man.

All the kids have had nose jobs
and the cat's booked in for a boob job,
but the gardener's making do with reiki and several flu-jabs.
My cocaine habit's coming on nicely
and the twins have made a blue movie – *so* hip.
Daddy's married our nanny – again – and
he'll be off to the Philippines
(once his heart can face the trip).

The dog has got his own Rolex
and the tax office can't smell a rat –
we trail our successes behind us
and the bank balance purrs like a cat.
We can't put a foot wrong. We've clawed our way up
through the school of soft knocks,
and that's that. We feel sorry for you
with your dope and your glue –
and your nose stud and weird rainbow hat.

We're doing so bloody, appallingly, awfully well –
don't you just hate us to absolute hell?

Eight o'clock in Britain

It's always eight o'clock in Britain.
No matter how you try and avoid it – it looms.
Like Groundhog Day.
It's always too late to *go* anywhere, *do* anything.

(Friend – it's too late not to do it, go there.)

In Barcelona, Paris, Rome they'll be promenading.
We walk round Huddersfield, Halifax, Hades and Hull –
we get the train to Doncatraz, across to York,
then down to Epping, Reading, Rhyl –
it's eight o'clock and the country has closed.
May as well be Knocking on Heaven's Door.
(Ever feel you've been here before?)
It's eight o'clock and growing late –
it's later than you think, mate.

Everywhere the same story.
Lights on in one kebab stop –
served by a yellow-eyed dog called Delaney,
the owner, asleep in the Back of the Shop.
Everyone's on drugs. *That* drug –
The 'Sod you. We're closed. Closed and you can piss off, pal' drug.
The 'Bog off abroad, if you're that bloody bothered.
We don't do promenades round here', mainline stuff.
Nah – we do the *Racing Times* and *Nuts* blowing round the city centre.
We do four lads in hoodies that look older than me dad
eating chips. And two lasses – pretending to be coquettish but really
only after t'chips.
It's eight o'clock and Britain has switched off, is in shutdown,
    meltdown, crackdown,
backdown, blowndown, growndown, thistledown, eiderdown,
    walkaround
pissed town.

It's eight o'clock and get yourself indoors – because
we don't do promenades round here – if you want that sort of crap
piss off abroad. That's more your thing (you look the type).
It's eight o'clock and we've got glass slippers on our feet.
It's eight o'clock in Britain – and growing late.

Ain't that right?
It's later than you think, mate.

All you need is love

There is no 'of course' about love.
There is no boat you cannot land,
no truth you cannot understand,
there is no 'of course' about love.
There are no grey jagged rocks,
no only black and white –
only a hand reaching out to make it all alright,
out, out of the depths.
There is no barking dog to pass by,
only a stray cat with no tail –
and you stood by the door, wondering how best to explain
what you cannot explain.
There is no 'of course' about love.
There is no easy Cluedo explanation,
no hammer in the hall, Miss Scarlett,
no revolver in the library being the reason why
Professor Pigeon had to die –
there is no spike you can remove with simple tweezers from the heart –
there is no elephant in your eye,
no badgers living in your feet,
there is no definite way to assure the people that you'll meet
that there is no 'of course' about love. Oh, no.
There is no map of your future,
no guarantee of sunny days –
but no reason in the world from hopes and dreams
to look the other way.
There is always tomorrow, no matter where you are.
No matter how thin your spirit's stretched,
there is no happiness you cannot catch,
there is no bad day that lasts forever,
there is a better way to be if
we all shine a light, together. Because
all you need is love. Love is all you need.

There is no door too small,
no bar that can't be raised – because
all you need is love
of course you do –
you can't kid me, pal –
I see right through you.
I wish I didn't, but I do.
There is no of course about love –
the sweet impossible saving ways of it –
the undeniable light-filled days of it –
the mysterious hopeful ways of it –
love is all you need –
love is all you need –
love is all *we* need.

Sixties Anthem

If I remember correctly
it was the summer we wore dahlias
in our hair from my uncle Ted's garden – he never knew
until years later that we were the culprits that scalped the earth. It
    was the summer that
we hitched a ride to Leeds and smoked dope with two truck drivers
until we were so stoned we pretended to be runaway trainee nuns
who the Pope was about to excommunicate because we had worn
    suspenders.
Visible suspenders. And then being dropped off at my aunt
    Chrissie's house
and her lying dead drunk on the floor from the beer affliction
and all and a man calling round with her new budgie and us taking
    it away with us
him not being keen at leaving it in the Guinness-dark parlour
where her head was wedged against the bathroom door.
Like an old dishcloth you said.
Except her hair was red, I thought.
Like Scarlett O'Hara – a great wounded Scarlett O'Hara.
And us dangling the budgie over the edge of the Bar Walls where
    we believed
there was a better place for him to fly to, and the bird screaming
    and calling
out like there was no tomorrow.

But there always was a tomorrow. It was just
today and yesterday that were in doubt.
If I remember correctly.

Baxter's Crime

Baxter, the dog, is being dragged down the lane.
Again.
I feel sorry for Baxter, in fact, most days –
I feel a bit like him.
Pulled this way and that.
Someone behind me with a lead that I can't see.
Baxter has no idea what his crime is.
(Nor have I.)
Just that he is a dog who takes his time, perhaps.
He investigates. Sniffs too long in all the wrong places.
I can never hear the words – just that she is shouting,
snapping and snarling.
I imagine the teeth are bared – the hackles grizzly and raised.
But Baxter I feel is undeterred.
He will go on being Baxter.
He will go on going on.

There is no cure for being free of mind and will.
Baxter, my friend, my alter ego.
Baxter – I love you.
Go on being, Baxter.

(Run amok – remain a dog with pluck.)

You bark at your side of the wall
and I will bark at mine.

The Kindness of Dogs

You say it and it is true.
Dogs are kind.
They buy small dog treats for each other.
They hold doors open for cats.
They run rings around the moon,
bury the sun in the sand and throw sticks
for the stars.
Dogs are kind.
They put paws on your knees on bad days.
They hold a light out to you in their eyes.
They run to the top of the mountain and bark
'Which stone did you want? Which one?'
and race back down with it and place it gently at your feet.
Dogs are kind (you say it and it is true).
They bark in all the right places at the theatre and hide
behind the sofa in the scary movie. They share their ice cream
with you, no questions asked.
Our dog – Zorro – the one we have not met yet
will be our best chum, best in the whole world.
He will be faithful and strong.
In dreams he runs right up to me, barks and says:
'You look a little peaky, why not take a year off
and come with me to Zanzibar. Stretch your legs and chase
your tail. See all that world out there? It's yours for the asking.'
And he gives me one of his fleas as a token of goodwill.
Dogs are kind.
They run into the sea and look amazed that it is wet
but they do not take offence.
They love a through-breeze in their ears, hanging out of windows,
a breeze that says they're happy in all the different continents.
Dogs are good map-readers and they always
know a better route – past the poodle beauty parlour and turn
right at the Dog and Duck.
Dogs lay their heads beside you and know just what you're thinking.
Dogs' favourite word is walk.
Dogs are kind.

Distance

What is it? How should I call it?
This distance that holds not you –
rather you hold it.
Yet, if you were here, this distance
would be gone – as it is it has no colour
nor sound – only a memory of you.
In its shape you lie, an invisible inked
horizon.

The dust lies here too, as thick as thoughts,
like some foreign perfume,
impenetrable as the dreaming sea.
There is a new room between us –
it is a garland of possibilities. It grows
as you sleep. It judges I cannot reach you.
Each day more dust settles.
Each day in the new room, the pages are turning
in a book, by an open window, and there
a butterfly sits, its small pulse in the sun's light.
The music of all we said goes on.

for Dad, with thanks

A wheelchair goes into a bar

A wheelchair goes into a bar and
conversation stops
and people remember somewhere else they have to be like
Doncaster or Iraq –
a wheelchair goes into a bar
and voices are lowered because maybe
this is how them bastards caught the plague
just by being near *it*... a wheelchair
goes into a bar
and it's like a time traveller has come in –

one from the planet
'fucking hell, wouldn't want to be them'
and the air absents itself
and the flowers on the tables get removed
('cause, why would you?) – when
a wheelchair goes into a bar.

A wheelchair goes into a bar, right –
and everyone cares, but no one looks
and there's obstacles called chairs
and people who will move
(preferably into another world)
and people who won't
and people who say
'I didn't know they came out at this time of night' –
and – 'that bloody man's caught my tights' –
oh yeah, a wheelchair goes into a bar.

A wheelchair goes into a bar
and if it's in Italy – people run out of the bar
and laugh, and carry you in and say you must be the Pope,
and if it's in France – people shrug their shoulders, cry,
tell you their life story and buy you cognac,
and if it's Ireland –
the bar is full of four-hundred other wheelchairs each with
a stranger story than yours, so at least you feel ordinary –

and if it's Prague –
fifteen musicians, four monkeys and twelve art students
bring the bar *outside* to you.
Oh yeah. A wheelie goes into a bar.

A wheelchair goes into a bar
and just wants a bloody drink.

The Open Door

Stories are what make us who we are.
Stories are what make the blackbird sing, what make
a friend call by – what keep the open door ajar.
Stories are what get me through, what keep me
able to go on. (Some days, only just.)
So, my love – let's tell each other stories.
Stories make up 98% of my body – the other 2%
is chocolate mixed with hope.
A bird flies in through my open door – he tells me
he has word from you.
It seems you're doing okay – but you miss me.
In the bird's beak, you have sent a rose,
like those my father grew and those my mother loved –
the wildest roses from the lane.
I miss you too. I miss our story.
The one we told together every day.
You holding me – always my happy ending.
This bird is freedom and he beckons.
Come, he says, *let me take you to him – tell one last story.*
This small bird – how he suns himself by the open door.
No cage for him.
Freedom, only freedom in his eye and in his plumage.
The air, she smells of roses, and the crescendo of his flight.
My love, there is one last story, under the sun
and I am called to tell it now.
We are the stories that we tell not with our mouths but with our
  hearts.
Imagine. The beauty of it.
Flying with that bird.
Imagine.

The Lucky Dip Machine of the Magic Bird of Fortune

And it reached out that long arm
at the fairground
into the shiny glass globe that was almost
as baffling and mysterious as the world itself –
and it reached out and into a shimmering, bobbling sea of blue teddy bears
and dogs with funny faces and sherbet dips and candyfloss key rings and star-
spangled clowns and angels with wands made of all my heart desired –
and found *you*.

And straight away – it knew what to do.

It defied gravity and sod's law (as well as a few others)
and it dipped down deep as if it was
hoping against hope and against all the odds
and because of all the reasons that things just don't work out
or that two people just miss each other by a second or two in the ether
and then they have to keep on going without each other
but always wondering and pretending
how life might have been –
and after a few near misses the silver arm came up for air

and with it there was *you*.

Staring out at me from the other side of the glass world
and you looked as baffling and mysterious as the world itself
(who could wonder, with only the clowns to talk to).
And the lucky dip machine spoke and said –
'Take him home – this one here.'
And down you came – down the shiny glass chute
like magic, right into my arms.
And me, that never had much luck before, had to pinch myself to see
    if it was true.

But the glass globe of mystery and the crazy bird of fortune had
    spoken.
And the clowns waved you goodbye
and the angels flew.

My Mother, the Mustang

How it reminds me of you, that horse language.
That other being who stands at the far edge of the field.
Myself, seven heartbeats away – and you pawing at the earth.
My mother, the mustang – the language of the mustang
a wild snatch upon the air.
In those last days, although you lay quietly
I know you saw everything as always, from the corner of your eye
and – the lips moved slightly when I came into the room.
Sat by your bed – you said: '*I'm* alright, more to the point, how are
    you?'
And then no answer, only a turning and a shifting of the head, a
    soft brush
of the mane against my hand.
The language of the steppes was yours – the running wild, the quiet
    grazing
and then the moving on. The wilderness calling you and you so
    very glad
to go. You cannot tame a mustang.
Why would you even want to?

How it reminds me of you,
that other language that I never learnt to speak.
Only sitting by the bed, giving water to the lips
bending low slowly to whisper in your ear, my love.
Thinking how fine the cheekbones that I've seen a million times,
    and the hazel
Irish eyes – closed, but still they see me.

Breathing in through my stomach deeper and deeper
so that all your fears dissolve. The language of the mustang, always it
    was yours.
I watch you step softly, nearer to me – just one word to leave me with
before the moving on. That world you have longed for and dreamed of
where the spirit takes you to run free as free.
I see a group of your kin are gathering by the bed and with them
fear dissolves, and the breath in my body is almost gone with you.
The sound of your leaving, mother, I know I will not hear –
just the sound of a river where it runs past the mountains
and the ground all around rich with hooves.

What They Found in the Poet's Stomach

What they found in the poet's stomach
was a dislike for bullshit on all levels.
A dislike for bullshit and a need to *declaim* that dislike.
They found a hatred of injustice and the gagging of freedom,
and the remains of several futile wars in the oesophagus.
It seems likely that they had drunk from the extremes
of poverty and calamity – and there was a residue of
famine and frailty in the bones – as if to know these
things would be to end them.
(Would that this were so.)
But mainly, overall – from Shelley to Keats, from Donne
to Dickinson to Plath to Byron and all the rest –
they found in the stomach lining itself – embedded in the gut –
the need for truth and the need for truth as beauty itself.
And this, without doubt, mi lord
was the actual *cause* of death, of each and every poet
whose names are writ in water, stone and blood,
and still they write.

Keats in Piazza Navona

All life, all love, all laughter is here
in Piazza Navona
where the waiters look like film stars
and the film stars look like waiters, where the birds
in the trees have golden feathers and the water in the
fountain is the water of life.
Yes, it's true – and in the middle of it all – sits Keats
and he is become well again – with the throb and sparkle
and urgency of life. He is writing and reading, reading and writing.
   People crowd him to listen to the poems
and they bring him pizza and they bring him wine and he
writes up a storm of poems. And then
Fanny joins him, she shimmy-dances across the square,
like some silver gypsy girl – she dances
and Keats feels the poems rise up from his feet and burst
out through his soul and they dance with the gypsy girl.
And the men and women in the square sing and dance with
happiness for Keats.
'You are not just a memory,' they shout, 'you are here with us now…'
and the poems become silver fish that rise and dance in the fountain
  – and the golden-feathered birds make an arc above his head
and myself sits and marvels – like a child at his feet.
All of life bursts out like spring from the earth in Piazza Navona
and Keats is become well again, at the heart of it.

Watcher of the Skies

When they tell you I am gone –
do not believe them.
But rather I am simply lost in space.
I am the new planet you cannot see – there,
where the purple comet hides behind the old moon.
My coat is made of the stars and my shoes of the sun.
I hoped it would come to this.
I dreamed it would come to this.
When as a child the skies drew me in, and the gentle
orb of my soul saw I had friends – they could not
stop me watching. I would not leave.
Sometimes at night I would stand alone and breathe in
the Universe, the whole of it, all its joys and sorrows.
Like a King, the night sky, and then the gentle Queen of the dawn
as the blackbird sings his heart away.
There is no poetry that can capture the sky, as the moments turn
into green surrender to Earth's delight.
Though I will try to enslave the sky with words
I cannot succeed.
This is every poet's task – to watch the skies.
And to leave them as they found them.
Dazzling as the blackbird's song.
And free as life itself.

The Romany Ghosts of My Father

They say –
'we'll see you when we see you, but for now
let's go travelling.'

They are here again –
the Romany ghosts of my father.
Always they wonder what's out there –
what lies beyond.
The Call of the Wild Blue Yonder – the Open Road.
Things to do – places to go – people to see –
a man about a dog…
(Do you like dogs?)

They say –
'what in the name of God are you doing *inside*?
Is that any way for one of our *own* to be?
Come on, now – let's go travelling.
Hang the pots and hang the pans
and go hang all the rest –
just the feel of the sun on your back and your two hands
grappling with eternity – just think –
What May or May Not Happen
Cannot Happen in the One Place.
Life needs movement,'
say the Romany ghosts of my father.

'Alright then – pack a few things, if you must.
Pack a squirrel, and a ginnel, a soup-opener and a cat –
even a hat – but *let's* go…
pack a song for your heart on an old hand-cart,
pack a mystery moment,
pack a mad March hare – if you dare – but
let's be off – before the day breaks,
before the last road calls, before the magic is gone,'
say the Romany ghosts of my father.

'Alright then, pack nothing – except laughter and long days –
and just keep walking (and spieling and talking)
and walk right out that door, feel your feet upon the Road, the
   Blessed Road.
Ah, sure – *going* – that's the thing
that keeps you warm, keeps you alive.
Be the Road – we are the Road –
the Open Road that lies ahead.
You don't need walls – ah no, you don't need anything.

Except. The stars above your head
(it has always been this way).
Moving on – a different place, a better place.
The fair's in town – no, it's the circus has come –
and we're the boys to help you ma'am…
we'll build the Big Wheel –
we'll even build the carousel –
(but tell the boss to go to hell)
we go our own way when the Road outside comes calling.'

The Romany ghosts of my father,
they will never let me be. Sometimes
it's midnight – and sometimes it's just before dawn –
and they whisper –
'Come on – will you come on now –
while the day, and the house and the world itself are sleeping
let's away – while there's still time and breath in your body
and hope in your heart –
pack nothing – except your good self –
for the Road outside – listen, listen well –
she is calling. Oh yes – she is calling.'

The Green Piano

Do not count the days, but rather *live* them.
Live them as if your next breath was a shipwreck,
as if your next heartbeat was the centre of a storm.
See that the pot of dreams does not stand empty and
mend all your many wars with your many selves.
Go everywhere. Do everything.
Show a little kindness – even to yourself.
Do all of this by Wednesday and
play always a green piano in your mind.
Play it as if your life depends on it which,
by the way, it does.
Set the table and eat there with someone you love.
Walk the enchanted city and walk it well.
Do not collect time in a match box.
If you come to a dead-end, laugh and walk on.
Eat midnight between two slices of bread.
If your cat won't sing, don't force him.
If there are only five questions in the world, never learn the answers.
And play always that green piano in your mind.
And know your life depends on it – so *play*.

Starting Over

We will start over again.
All of us. This is my belief, always has been.
From the bottomless pit of my daydreams, I know this to be true.
I am not a badly-worked engine, simply a car that has gone off the rails.
There will be somewhere where Hoovers and headaches and hand me downs and
hurricanes – have no place. They cannot get a purchase.
They slide the slippery slope to nowhere – and there is simply – peace.
A wilderness of peace. A desert of peace.
And I will no longer be a car. I will be anything I desire –
and it will change every day. And it will not matter – no not even the small things.
There will be ginger beer flowing in the fountains.
There will be a city run by wolves who can outrun the wind. I will be a wolf
making my way down a great hill at such a speed that no one and nothing can catch me.
There will be moonlight to eat and some left over to dance by.
And there will be such wonders to see within the gates of the city that my breath
will stop then start again for joy itself.
And there will be people I have loved on every street corner – waving and laughing
and saying – 'we tried to let you know, but it's as if you couldn't hear us, your old friends.
Our voices were lost in the green air – though we called often when we saw your need was greatest.'
Yes, they will take me by the arm – and all the time in between will be a shadow, a memory and
through the gates of the city I will go.
And though I'll call often – through the green air to where you, my love, are battling –
you also will not hear me. Though I will call all the days of my life – all the days of your life – until
you are come to the gates of the city and we are done with this shadow dance.

— from *Americana* (2015) —

The letter that never came for the old song and dance man

It was always that letter.
The one that he remembered – the one that never came.
That said:
'Come, Billy. Come to America.'
It said:
'Everything you've ever dreamed of is here.
So – come.
Uncle Pa and Aunt Rose are grand – and the baby is fit and well and strong.
God be praised.
Can you believe we even have somewhere to live.
Even ma has a job at the bakery – they are rich in life here and the days
are a sight warmer and the nights don't kill you.
Land can belong to you here, and you to the land.
So come.'
The letter that never came to the old song and dance man.
The letter you always remembered opening, dad.
Would have opened in a heartbeat, in a second. Like a magician.
A man with a future. A man with luck on his side and a song in his heart.
Doing the soft shoe shuffle in a place called Brooklyn, what you dreamed of.
'There are so many of our own here, Billy – but
it's as if they seem to know us, to understand that all we want
is a place to lay our heads and our dreams. Can you believe it, Bill?
Believe it.
This is a place you can walk tall and not be short of a bob or two.
The boat – hah – that was another matter – sure I thought Pat was a gonner.
It took all of the strength that Kilmartin and I possess to see him through.

Sometimes the worst of a storm is both terrible and necessary and
   has to be done.
And that is where you find us now – the other side of the storm.
Kilmartin and ma, and Rose and the children
and myself John Burke and your uncle Patrick Rowan.
We think of you every day, Billy – and I am sending this letter as
   promised.
Leave all of that other nonsense behind, Billy – you were made for
   this country
and it for you.
So, pack nothing except the hopes and dreams you stand up in.
We will be waiting right where the storm ends and freedom shakes
   your hand.
Where the life that is yours by right – is waiting for you.
Ma says – 'tis a grand life – if you don't weaken!
So just come Billy – just COME.'

Route 66

Tired and jet-lagged, our first day in America
friends propped us up next to Route 66, and said,
'there, you have arrived. This is America.
Land of the Free.'
But, we could hardly keep awake, and what's worse
there was no sign of Jimmy Cagney.

The Cakes at Walts

The cakes at Walts are huge – no, bigger than that.
They loll about the counter like disgruntled teenagers.
They don't look you in the eye, too busy texting
the pastry counter for more cream.

People bring wheelbarrows to ferry them home as if
they were drunks. Drunks with big chocolate eyes
and angelica frosted mouths.
'Stay back. There has been a cookie violation.
One of the cookies contains real chocolate.'
How has THIS happened?
One of the kids from Homewood being clever, I guess.
The counter is awash with their big, whipped faces.
Once they were lean and mean and hard,
but today is the 4th of July and a lot of Red Bull has flowed
under the river since then.
They sink their teeth into children's arms, if they don't like
the look of them. They fight over who gets the stars and stripes
Dayglo stand with matching flag.
When we get to the front, there is just a pistachio dinosaur
and a strawberry unidentified flying object left.
We both know, it's got to be the dinosaur and soon we come
to blows with a six foot guy and his three kids.
But then, he hears our British accent and decides to be kind.
So we wheel our dinosaur down to the checkout
even though it snaps and snarls and it leaves a syrupy trail
like some weird obese, high cholesterol snail.
This is America, where cakes are large enough to feed an army.
Just the one cake we have, could double as a country.
'I want therapy,' the cake shrieks. 'Get me some therapy
and some toothpicks – and get 'em NOW.'
When we get back – Mel and Mike say –
'We told you so, but would you believe us? No, you would not.'
And we give the cake its own room with its own air con.
And the promise of a Yale education. Well –
it's the 4th of July – what can you do?
You got to let them eat cake. Any sort of cake.
Just as long as it's Walts – and it's Huge, Huge.
Huge.

The Basement Kids

The basement kids, with their basement smiles
live very different lives to us.
They drink basement coke, eat basement popcorn,
bang on massive basement drums.
We don't have a basement, you said – wistful.
Let's show you ours, they say.
And down you go into their mad purple crazy wild
simmering shimmering astroturf hasta la vista
basement world.
There are kids lolling on couches eating pizza –
some have been there all week.
Forgot to go home. We are stardust, we are golden,
one whispers in your ear – wild laughter follows
everything in the basement.
The walls are made of broken rules and the ceiling
is old computer parts and songs that automatically
burst forth when you turn on the basement lights.
The lights are made of dancing iguanas.
The floor is covered in metro tickets and old exam results.
We don't have a basement, you say – as if you
have no God.
They let you sit a whiles on the red couch they keep
for grown-ups.
Their faces have assumed that look that tells you nothing. Zero.
    Zilcho.
You realise they are waiting for you to go.
You stand up – they rap dance you to the exit.
When the door closes – you hear the basement birds
begin to sing again.
You climb the stairs – there are other adults there.
They make you tea – and say calming things and
you know you'll pull through.
Under the floor you all feel the pounding,
the distant heartbeat, start.

Fireflies in Melanie's Garden

They write words in the night air and we
poor fools, do not catch them.
These are my first fireflies, and I am their first poet.
'Poet what will you write about us?' one sings –
and someone catches it – holds it in their hands
so I can see it better.
Small yellow stars full of
conversation and memory and meaning.
Fallen stars? Fallen pieces of stars?
I cannot say.
Only that I do not want them caught, held captive as I am.
No. Let each be at one with the night sky, with the rose bush they
    settle on, let them dive and alight where fate sends them.
Let it sing – and let me not understand it.
Melanie holds a jar of them aloft – they sway inside
the small cage like Sinbad sailors sensing the storm.
'What is poet' – the one at the front sings – and I can
give no answer. I want to say – a poor man's firefly.
Looking down at my body
I see I am turning into a firefly, pulsing and golden.
I feel no weight, no worries, no troubles, and yet
still my wings are caught by the world.
'Poet – you are one of us', they sing with one voice! And as they fly
    up to and beyond
the indigo of the world's roof, I see how freedom may
be claimed again – and YES –
I fly with them. My whole body is become alive again.
Below me – I see surprised faces – and an empty cage.

'I think she got a good view,' Melanie says.
'Yes, really, quite a good view.'

Racoon Runs for President

To explain it better – Mike brings two skulls out.
See, the racoon, he says – he could run for President,
quite a cute cookie, all round. BUT.
Then, we have the possum – and although he means well,
he's not going anywhere. Except maybe the beach.
Look, I want to say – most of the people at school with me,
were possum graduates.
And they did OK.
Sure, one or two had a little extra tuition, but so what?
Now, the racoon, Mike continues – he knows
whose paws to grease, which garbage bin to empty
and on whose driveway. So, if he were to be elected,
we can see where he's going with this.
The two skulls sit side by side on the table, eyeing each other up.
The possum looks lost in thought, while the racoon –
he always has an angle, that's for sure.
The racoon is always waiting until he retires to go fishing.
But, the possum? He just goes fishing.
I know who I'd vote for.

Bob Goes for Popcorn

Bob goes for popcorn – and he says,
'You can get a refill from the hanging garden
of popcorn on the wall'
and I think – so, I really must be in America.
Then he orders a chilli dog – (I don't know
what this actually is) and I think – of course,
this is what you eat when you are in America.
Which is where I must be.
We came in off the street – hot enough to fry an egg on,
into Jay B's bar on the corner of Hanover and Main.
That's what they say here.
I was hoping for at least one cowboy hat on someone
propping up the bar – but no one obliges.
I order a dog too – but my dog is almost bigger than me.
Two waiters are needed to carry it.
Then Bob goes for popcorn and we watch the Bears on TV
that floats over the bar.
We ask the waitress to take a photo.
She is called Kitty – and takes three photos because I
just ain't smiling enough.
This is because my dog has overwhelmed me.
It should be on a leash.
You order a Bud – and we pretend we are
almost American.
Then we go back out to the hot dusty street
that is like a white rodeo of heat.
And on we ride.

The Chicago Drug Guy

He asks us if we got the time,
but Mike says – no – he's really asking if you want cocaine.
Then he asks 'how are you today?'
but Mike says – no – he is asking if you were followed.
He thinks we are someone we ain't.
And we smile like simple monkeys and say
we don't have a watch on, and we are very well.
He shoots me a look that chills my spine.
He is tall and broad and you wouldn't want to argue with him
in an alley. (Or anywhere…)
He looks like we upset him now.
His jaw is clamped on the air and he pulls his hat well down.
'Do ya got the time or what', he says –
then a man comes up in a check shirt and says
'Hey, yo talking to me, bro,'
and we are in the park waiting for the Beethoven to start
but they don't look like Beethoven fans.
But you never can tell.
When the music starts – it's never clear where you'll end up.

That Lady Liberty

She picks you out – that Lady Liberty,
picks you out from birth. Says – this is your lot,
your allocation – this is your link in the chain.
For you are also, the forest, not just the tree.
Does she have her reasons – that Lady?
Why that little bit of freedom – will it not stretch
to everyone? Bring all humanity into play.
The freedom to speak out – in places crushed;
the freedom to be yourself – denied. And dangerous.
Look – throw a bottle in the sea – with words of hope for all,
see if it floats, and if it too is free.

What do we ask of freedom?
Just a share of all that's fair and good and true and strong.
That Lady Liberty, she has a lot to answer for.
One day – when I see her face to face – sail in at that other shore,
I am poised to ask all that was meant.
And answer I will have.
For I am leaf, as well as tree, as well as forest.
And answer I will have – where that other freedom waits.
Until then – like you – all I can do is ASK.

The Cuban Lady

She is blonde, about sixty, very pretty.
She has been a dancer she tells us.
Her old trolley she takes everywhere – 'I'll get ya
a cawfee,' she says – and goes in search.
'I been visiting my daughter, she lives uptown.'
She asks what is wrong with me, and we laugh.
Survival is all about laughing in the face of crap.
How true, she says, how true.

So, what's the deal New York?

New York – is a poet.
No, it's a troubadour – its Blondel –
it's a carousel.
No... it's none of these.
I see it now – New York is a butterfly.
Gold on Staten Island, blue on Manhattan and
scarlet red on Long Island.
You cannot pin it down, the butterfly that never sleeps.
It has a thousand different colours, fourteen kinds of birdsong
and a dance you can't identify.

It moves in herds of butterflies across the open land.
It is golden in the night and is hidden by the light.
See – a million dreams ignite as it lands on the Brooklyn Bridge.
New York has these wings that you think you almost see –
as it lands on your arm – it's a carousel, a clown – as you
climb into bed – see it's even made me rhyme – think I had all
the time in the world – which I don't. I see now NY is a butterfly.
That never ever sleeps.

Empire State Violation

We are in a violation, and this is a shooting offence.
We stood too near to the elevator.
We were eating a cookie at the time, a cider doughnut
extra sugar, and now we are in a violation.
The cop has got a weapon trained on us – it could be
a man or a woman – he or she has a moustache and very shiny shoes.
'Move away from the elevator, Sir. Move away.' The gun is aimed
right at your head. All around people are panicking.
Several schoolkids are filming it on a mobile phone.
A small child with ringlets – pulls at someone's skirts –
'When's daddy coming home, marmy?'
The floor is shiny too, little pieces of mosaic that are
full of inscriptions about liberty and freedom and the nearness
of justice.
Our cookie is taken from us, we are taken to a small room.
They say the view from the top is remarkable, the best there is.
But we are in a violation – what with standing too near to
the cop's shiny shoes. And what's more – they keep the doughnut.

In Which I Dream of Rats

All the kids in New York, are looking after rats.
Old ones, young ones, shiny ones, tatty ones –
they fatten them up, keep them in their breast pocket
like beady-eyed pocket watches, pointy little teeth.
This is my best one – he is truly awesome, little Bono says.
All of the kids in Queens, and Brooklyn and the kids who no one knows
that run round Central Park –
are looking after rats.
Handsome ones, dog-eared ones, chunky ones big as French fries
with dewy donut eyes, and thin ones no bigger than the man
who digs through the garbage down on Seventh Avenue.
And the rats say stuff – like –
'All they gave me was a lousy thousand dollar raise, they can
stick it up their ass' – and –
'What do you hear, what do you say?
What do you do and what do you make?'
The rats smoke outside buildings and the smoke rises and fills
the air like plumes on the cop's horse who waits patiently
for life to pass. Faces the traffic, and is called Mercedes.
All of the New York kids are googling and texting and keeping close
to rats. Grinning ones, leering from the sidewalk ones,
chocolate chip cookie eating violation ones, toting great big
gun ones and cramming down a cheeseburger ones.
Where are they coming from? And it's best you should know
you are never more than six feet from a kid in New York City.
I – HEART – New York. (So weird they named it, twice.)
And – all the rats are keeping kids.
The kids are growing tails
and the rats are walking taller, kinda sassy and upright.
You know what I'm saying?
Who is keeping who? The day is so hot, I can't tell anymore.
My body is melting into the sidewalk.
My soul is made of dollars, my rat translates it into pounds.
I – HEART – New York. New York, New York.
So weird they named it. Twice.

Pushing

Everyone in New York is pushing something.
Guys are pushing mysterious boxes.
Women are pushing racks of handbags.
Clowns are pushing their feet along pavements.
Dogs are pushing cats to the sidewalk.
Mice are pushing their way down to the river.
Bus drivers are pushing Chinese students up to the top deck
and evicting wheelchairs.
Taxi drivers ain't pushing nothing, nowhere, no way, no how.
Pimps are pushing their best girls to smile.
Garbage hunters are pushing food into their mouths.
Dream sellers in the park are pushing the idea of all things dark.
Irish pubs are pushing Dublin Bay prawns into Chicago rolls.
Old Jewish guys are pushing huge candelabra.
Mickey Mouse is pushing Minnie – he just found out that she earns
   more than him.
The priest is pushing his gun in the face of the drug dealing jogger,
   while he waits for the nun to put the cuffs on him.
The lost tourist is pushing the hot pavement of Central Park
under his feet, while he asks the bored doorman chewing gum,
   'Was it here that John died?'
The lake in the park is pushing at the edge of the city – and the
   white horses so tastefully groomed are pushing themselves not to
   scream and go mad.
The Sicilian hot dog vendor who fries you an extra egg – is
pushing himself not to remember a quiet grove in Italy where
his mother still lives.
The Polish waitress who walks the streets at night is pushing herself
   not to hate you.
The people at the Happy Clappy Church are pushing themselves
   just to love, love, love you.
The beetles on 54th Street are at war with the ear wigs on 56th
   Street.
The rats are heading down to the river with the mice, except for a
   solitary rat who thinks, BELIEVES, he can make it on Broadway.

We are pushing the boundaries of all we believe, thought we
    believed. (But that was before we came here.)
We hold each other tight. Pull each other up high, onto a tiny
    ledge, that overlooks this madhouse.
Pushing. Pushing.
Everyone in New York is pushing. Something.

The John Lennon Doorman

He is savvy. Smart as a whip, and savvy.
He has gypsy eyes and a sulking mouth that chews gum
and he has stood here now for too long, too many hours.
A minute in New York is a year in anyone's language.
We ask him – 'Is this where it happened? Is this where
they shot Lennon?' – the words freeze in the air.
He chews the gum, real slowly. Adjusts his gold buttons
with the arrogance of a lord, checks his reflection in his shoes.
(On the anniversary day, he makes sure he gets time off.)
'See, I'm in a band – been in a band all my life – my wife
she's an actress – and yet, no one comes here asking about us.'
'So they shot some guy. This is New York – what were you expecting?
    – this ain't no Disneyland, this ain't no picnic in the park.'
And his breath freezes in the air above his head.
And the flames burn real high behind him – like a gold message left
    by some guy.
And we shiver, and I ask you for my gloves, and we walk on.

A Few Dollars More

Here in the dangerously warm burden of the night
where the freeway meets the interstate line –
small flying creatures are landing in my hair.
I get up, I brush them off,
they come back.
The shadows of the game go on all night.
You say – don't be afraid – there's no reason to be.
There's nothing out there – except the night.
(That's exactly my point.)
A woman in the next door room is screaming,
calling out – for a bagel, for a different man,
for a few dollars more. For the moon.
Yeah, I tried that one too.
Anything to take away the lousy pain.
There is a knock on the door, her door.

Seems like they brought her the bagel.

Heatwave, Rhode Island

This heat is Rothko hot,
full of anguish and interpretation
of our waking lives.
This heat is a challenge, each day we approach it
like breathless warriors – poking toes out
into the air.
You see blocks of hopeful colour,
you move towards it – in an instant
it is gone. And,
you are left – hot. Jambalaya hot.
Crescendo hot. Hades hot.
Red to the touch, crimson, our touch on the world.
You wake – and say – 'Hey, you getting up or what?'
And it's another day.

Joleen, Joleen

Joleen is our room cleaner, we meet her in the lift
as we are going down, she is coming up.
She says –
I'll be down directly and see to y'all for breakfast.
What do you want. Do you want grits?
When we get down, she is there,
apron on and squeezing oranges with her feet,
while dusting the tables and cleaning the windows.
I ain't never been outside of here, she smiles – it's mighty
fine here, don't you think? We agree.
Tomorrow is my busy day, she says – I'se overseeing a funeral
of Old Mrs Benson, and then I has to take her dog to
the pound. He's called Dusty, and it's a real shame.
I'd take him myself, but Elmer is allergic to dog fleas.
What you want with your grits? Do you want grits with
your grits? Or do you just want grits?

The Man on Wickenden Street

We go into the shop. His record shop.
And he tries to look busy even though no one has
been in, in days. Except for a unicorn and
a chihuahua having a bad trip, thought it was a pizza palace.
We ask him about Frank Zappa – says he never heard of him.
We say what about Nick Drake? Joni Mitchell?
Now he thinks we're collecting for something.
Then his friend comes in – (he's met him twice on Twitter
so it counts) – and they high five for all of ten minutes
until the little guy gets groin strain.
We ask about his tattoos. All 15. He says what tattoos?
So, what have you got, we ask – and he has Snoop Diddy
and the Dangerous Dogs, and Munching Leroy Kiljoy
and the No Direction Monkeys.
We think we'll pass. We would have liked some early Doors
or a little Tim Buckley, maybe.
Now, a girl comes in with curly eyes and a permed smile.
She is an actress and has had motivational problems getting the
    door open.
We leave them all wrestling, in the sunny window, to see who is
more cool. (My money's on the chihuahua.)

Emily's Dress

Emily's dress stands at the top of the stairs
And you cannot catch its eye. Not directly.
It plays hide and seek with you – breaks free of the glass
and rustles all over the house.
'You seek me here, you seek me there
but she is everywhere.
I am not one for a glass case, so why have they stood
me there, like a living ghost?
I am more alive now, than ever I was.'

There is the sound of a huge dog running up the stairs –
and he too smashes the glass.
'Follow us. Follow us, to the woods quickly,
before the light fades.' And we do.
She is direct in her asking. Direct in her giving.
'I am a knuckleduster of a poet,' she whispers in the long
grass down by the stream.
'I am not the shadow of the white oak. Rather –
I am the white oak that survives the storm.'
In the woods she shows us mermaids seated at pianos and,
there, LOOK – is a tall dreaming-eyed giraffe.
'That is father,' she says.
'And the little white deer – that is mother.'
'My heart beats like the stars,' she says.
'How goes it with yours?'
And the clear crystal of her song becomes mine.
We own the same white dress, I say.
'Then do not let them stand you in a case,' she says.
'But always keep a dog to hand that you may break free.'
And the blue of the grass and the mermaids' singing
and the pianos in my feet – a quite overcome me.
'I am not going back,' she says. 'Not to that cage.
Not for anyone.'
And we drink lilac wine, and hang from the stars.
She is a guiding light, a shining light – this Emily.
The other half of the world is in my head, I say.
I must write it down.
I know, she says, I know.
Here is paper, I will help.
And, she does.

In Emily Dickinson's Garden

A butterfly, a white butterfly lands on my arm
and I think – ha ha – it's her, it's Emily.
But, no.
Then, out from the tall shadows a smaller shadow
runs before us. Beneath the white oak is where she lives, hides.
But today, she does not hide.
In the heat of the day that blusters and whinnies,
this is the Emily that likes to laugh and dance and sing.
The birds know her. The garden knows her.
This Emily is a cheeky racoon. A stripey racoon.
The flowers in the garden are all in bloom – captured and captivating.
There are roses and foxgloves, and sweet William and lilies –
and teazels – and – oh look, she says – look at the bandit flowers and
the will-o-the-wisps and the robber Chinese lanterns.
You may swing from them.
Look at their nightingale petals and coronet hearts and
the silent crescendo of the grass. Oh look.
And Emily shows us each of them in turn.
As racoons go, she is pleasant company.
I must confess, I say, I took you for the butterfly.
Oh no, she says, far too pale – and too far-fetched.
Although she stands with fourteen of them like a crown
around her head.
In the shade of her brother's white oak, we rest a while
and she shows me a piano-playing mermaid – one that
she called down earlier.
And Carlo? – he is with us of course.
A huge bounciness of goodness and trust and large paws.
My mistress is a racoon, he barks – and only we know why.
And he runs rings around the sun and settles at her feet.
And all, in all, with all – the dark world within my eye
becomes possible again. And light as birds of hope.
I am only here briefly. (We are all, just so.)
And at the far end of the garden I catch her morning eye
and smile. And she knows I must go.

But yet, we sit awhile amidst the honeycomb of air.
Quiet as bees and impossible as mermaids. Our sea-spun hands
and the honey of our song is all around.
And she wraps her stripey tail around my arm.
For truth is company.
And the darkness of the world recedes.
And I am whole. And I am glad.
The flowers stamp and wave and cheer.
And Emily is glad at heart
as I myself, take strength from her, am glad.

Americano Pizza

Tonight, we eat pizza like wolves.
Mad, bad, wild and dangerous to know, wolves.
English wolves.
Behind us is Providence, and the almost full moon
puts on a show. And the rainbow edge of the houses
against the water, takes our breath away.
Young couples along the bay discuss Plato,
and whether to call the first baby Antoine or Chereena.
The girl in the petrol station serves two dozen
condoms to a boy on a skateboard and says to us –
'Oreo cookies? I got a brother in law as black
as they.'
We walk back along the bay and the pizza growls
in its box, like a hunted owl.
Like a werewolf in drag.
Like an ocean of all new words in a lover's mouth.
We run like wolves and howl at the pizza moon.

Better Late Than Never

My dad is packing his suitcase for America
and nothing I say will stop him.
'But dad,' I say, 'you're dead. Just how do you plan
to do this? Hmm?' And he says, counters with,
quick as ever – as quick as the brown fox that outsmarts them
    hounds –
'Sure, a little thing like being dead never stopped me before.
When I was young, as you know, nothing stopped me.
When I was young and foolhardy, nothing stopped me.
When I was young, foolhardy and Irish and poor –
nothing prevented me in life, no, not a thing.
You're too easily deflected. Try and see death as
just another stamp in your passport – sure, that's the thing.'
And he continues packing.
His old brown razor, the little steel comb, his dancing shoes, the suit
    from Dublin
and the hat Aunt Sarah bought him, and the picture of his wedding
day – stood with mam and the whole of life ahead of them.
In they all go – and truth to say – he is ready way before me.
And it seems, he is right.
When we get to New York – they recognise him straight away.
And welcome him in – like a long lost ghost.
'We expected you a few years back, Billy – no matter.' And in he goes.
And the fact that we are with him?
Stands us in great stead. We are sent to the head of the queue.
Treated like royalty.
We look for him after Customs – and there he is –
telling stories to a group of mucky faced kids. Near the exit.
'I'll see youse later,' he shouts. 'I've to see a man about a filum
part first, and then Kelly and meself are going downtown – a couple
of bars and a whole lifetime of dreams with our names on them.'
And with that, he is gone. Into the New York air, that is a little wary
    of us,
but not him – him it knows to be absolutely one of its own.

And so, at last – with the sun shining down – my father finally
    made it to America.
Being young and foolhardy and Irish and poor. Even, dead.
No, none of this could, or dared to stop him.
Just think of death as another stamp on your passport.

— from the Origami Poems Project (2010-2016) —

The Whisper of Birds

This says it all – the whisper from the trees.
This morning, a magpie –
(the not so lucky bird, by whose decree?) –
who says which bird should by a single brighter feather
be the lucky one?
I want my words, my life to mean something
and nothing comes – except this bird –
sitting doleful-eyed staring in at me.
As ever he is on the wing.
Never resting, never knowing when his last day may come,
or what song he's best to sing.
My thoughts they come and go like the murmur of the trees.
The birds they whisper in their souls and so create the day.
What a piece of luck they are – even this magpie is soft as he
    watches over me.
He picks at the bread placed for him in the old tin.
His mind is set on seeking out a different tree where
no one will fear the whisper in his throat, his midnight words.
He's soon away.
And I am glad – for his little piece of luck.

The Russian Doll that Was My Mother

Like the Russian Doll we kept on the sideboard –
that was you, mam.
Foreign, exotic, that mysterious smile, unfathomable.
Your exterior of certainty, so hard won, over years.
(How many dolls since I saw you?)
For everyday, you used the first doll – she is tough and gruff.
Sometimes on birthdays and at Christmas
a second doll appears – kinder eyed and softer.
Then once, walking home – myself falling on the ice –
a further doll still, one who held me tight and said
'My Lass. My Own Lass – You they Must Not Break.'
And so we walked together on – through the dark eyed storm.
(How many dolls since I saw you?)
That last doll mam – her I never met nor even knew.
But what strange mystery she had – I know I learned the trick from
    you.
Dangerous the doll that gives too much away.
How many dolls since we walked through the storm?
How many? How many dolls?

Walking the Dog

Why should I speak of pain?
He does not speak of me,
but goes his own way, this dull dog.
There he goes, across tall iron gates.
Can you see him? Can you feel his icy tread?
When I try to pin him down you know
there is little of the green fields I have loved
about his eye. Today I will not go with him.
I will make him look away, for you know
he has no guts.
And his eye will lack courage at the last.

Beer

Beer is you. Beer is you Against All Odds.
Uttering the Great Truths of the Universe,
and me, listening.
Beer like you always lands on its feet.
It is a secret halved, a good woman, the one
you say you'll never meet.
Beer is a gold embrace and all that glitters.
It is where in the barmaid's lonely flat,
Joe the cat suns himself, in a single
billiard ball of light.

The Midnight Boat

The boat that bears your name, she is midnight.
The boat that you my mother took – and yet
I never saw it land.
Only caught the sound of it – myself stood at the door.
Heard the soft beat of a gull's wing as I held your hand,
then the rising into air – the two of you – the call of midnight's
    shore.
The picture on the wall behind –
a felucca setting sail – the gleam of the oars
and the waves that bear your name.
All that is, is beyond time and time itself – the key.
Flying high towards the boat – you are the joyful gull
and glad to go. I do not blame you – for such a boat, who
could bear to stay.
The midnight boat stands watchful on the shore.
The waves are quick as heartbeats and pull the oars around.
See, the white gull rises.
(Tomorrow – it's a lovely day.) And the midnight boat is gone.

The Moon Crying

It seems a strange sort of night to any other.
A night when friends can call to each other and remember,
hold each other close.
We notice the moon is crying, tear by tear.
The tears fall over the castle and down the hill.
My eyes cannot see all of the picture, though the moon hangs low
　　obligingly.
Someone brings out the wine, we stir it with jasmine stems.
The picture almost complete.
Only my heart hangs back. Only my heart says wait.
There are two moons tonight (the one watches the other).
We bring nothing but ourselves to this silent space, why, the moon
　　herself
has brought no more.
She is a silver guardian, a panther that walks before and behind us.
Which moon are we to believe?
Which moon is real? For, the moon never lies.
We follow the braids of her long black hair.
We ascend star by star, following her panther stride.
We take each separate moon as we find her – in the root of a tree,
in the hoot of an owl, in the thumbprint of dawn.
This crying moon is the moon in truth – and tonight as ever –
the moon never lies.

Bonsai

It came in a cheap box,
but, the thing itself
quite dear, I understand.
It would take years, they made that clear to us.
I was all for a nice geranium,
but, the idea of longevity drew you.
A little bit of immortality – and you were sold.

My cigarette burned strangely bright
as they unwrapped it, lovingly.
Already I vowed not to water it,
foolishly thinking I was giving it a chance.
It could live or die by its own devices,
this stunted seer of the ages.
The ash from my anger flops
into its saucer daily, and it thrives,
languid in its pebble-base
like some weird and ancient crane.
I tell you frankly, it makes me nervous.
Other plants wither, if placed too near.
My hands look pale beside it.
It has roots that lie beyond time's grasp.
It has seen too much and now it seeks revenge.

The Blind Dog

I do not want to answer the door.
I want to laze around with a bone
and not be first all the time.
No one asked me if I'm cut out for this –
which I'm not.
I have to wear a harness and a sign
that says don't talk to me.
Why couldn't she have been a footballer?
But running?
Makes me go dizzy watching them.
How does she even know if she's won?
I'm not allowed to bark in case it
distracts them.
This is no life for a dog.
I'm going to advertise –
get her a pony, a small one.
She'll never know.

The Littlest Hobo

I am the Littlest Hobo.
I am a stray, but not a runaway.
There was nowhere that I ran from.
I come into towns from the East and leave them from the West.
I find it's for the best.
The call of moving on is in my soul.
If I stay, I can't win. I know this to be true.
You may see me at your window;
I'll help you if I can.
No one owns me – I belong to no one,
neither woman nor man.
I board the train for Everywhere, just
when no one's looking. The call of all the different towns,
the stories of the people – I NEED to be there.
I need to see them all.
Wouldn't you, if you could? (Somehow, I think you would.)
I am the Littlest Hobo, I am a stray, but not a runaway.
There was nothing I ran from. No anger, no fear.
No one gives me home or shelter, I make my own way.
Watch out for me today and I'll help you if I can.
But, in the morning I'll be gone. (The answer's in the next town.)
Someone there has worries, so don't ask me to stay.
The answer's not with you.
My heart is my compass, my feet keep me true.
By the light of the moon, I arrive – with the dawn's first rays, I am
    gone.
The Littlest Hobo.
A stray, but not a runaway. Never a runaway.

The Leaves of Dachau

This is the language of leaves.
They who are gone
before they are gone.
'The moment you give in,
falling is forever,' they whisper.
Inside this one leaf
I can see – life is hanging on.
I can see it is arrogant.
I can see it is stubborn.
Even though the cold has come.
Even though the other leaves are in hiding.
It will not fail.
On these trees there is no room to sit, no place to breathe, to speak.
No chance to say goodbye, no farewell space.
Look. This is the place where they fall.
Their bones crushed into the cold earth.
Winter happens under the very eyes of spring.
Year after year, and still.
Nothing is done.
Just the black rage of buried leaves falling victim to the air.
Winter has a file on ice.
Autumn goes to the shelf, reaches down the dark book, interrogates each one.
There is a power of frozen words beneath the ice.
They are ours forever.
They who are gone. Before they are gone.
Where will it all end – this falling?
Mother by father. Sister by brother.
The voices resound in the earth.
Dying comes easily to leaves.
This sky holds the blood of them, season after season.
But, this one leaf, that is holding on.
It keeps something of the sun in the corner of its soul's eye.
There is a whisper they will not shake it.

The Last Time

The last time I saw my father I think we spoke about blackbirds.
The way they have no agenda, and in the snow are easy to spot.
The way they trust you will not harm them and in the middle of
   the afternoon
suddenly, a song occurs to them which they must sing.
I remember it was not a sunny day, but there was a light
playing through a window. Playing, as if it were a blackbird.
And I said – I'll write a poem for you, about the bird – and he said
with an air of using his words like a song, a melody he did not know,
that there would not be time.
Only that he would be thinking of me, when I wrote the poem.
And that the words might be mine – but the tune and all the
   melody were his
and his alone.
And at that moment, a blackbird came to the window.
And a song occurred to me – a rarity as I am not musical –
and from a distant room a melody I did not know began to play.
And turning back towards him – I saw no further joke nor wave.
And I sit and write the poem – fool that I am – with my little pot
   of words
and the melody – spectacular.

Two Dreams

Two dreams I had, and not sure which to believe.
In the first I am in a dungeon.
No way out ever, and can't get home.
There is the sound of my own blood being drawn
and metal in the air, a smell of sulphur.
The feeling I came there on a horse – and he too has not escaped.
I am in white and wield great power and all of this has been my
   downfall.
In the second dream – I am a dancer again, waiting
for my turn in the wings.

A blue billowing curtain stands before my face
and while I wait I write my name
over and over in the sand with my ballet shoes.
The music is sublime – and two old friends arrive
and argue as to who will dance with me.
They both say they will come back later,
but I know this will not happen.
This dance I wait to do is mine alone, a thing apart.
A lonely eagle calling out to air from the mountain
I have called my heart.
(There are promises we keep and cannot keep – even
in our dreams.)
Two dreams I had, and not sure which to believe.

Visiting the Parrot

Through the window I could see the small cage,
and his shape clutching at the edges of it.
She made us tea – the woman.
I have saved him, she said, *from definite destruction.*
If it weren't for me, she said, *where would he be?*
She let him out and he climbed sideways down
to have a good look at me. Leaning a little breathless
(that being the two of us) – I sensed a fellow clown,
an acrobat – squawking – only let them see what we want them to see.
Chintz wallpaper. Earl Grey in perfect white porcelain.
And the sky outside – beckoning.
And our two hearts like defused weapons.
He went a little dizzy with the sweetness of the air
(much as I do myself on good days)
Tell me, how goes it? we asked each other.
His head leaned on my shoulder before he climbed back in.
And the teacups rattled.
And through the window, I swear I saw and heard the sky itself –
I could feel the two of us – clutching at the edge of it.

What I Meant to Do

I had intended to look at the roses today, but
the rain fell and obscured my view and the Carpathian
Mountains would keep on invading the garden and a small dog,
name of Ginger, was sat on the window sill and all the time the
    rain fell.
And my view grew narrower and seemed further away, and the scent
of the roses, real and distant – no longer seemed real –
and I put the roses on hold and did not go out into the garden
in the pure beauty and haberdashery of the rain
and let the roses take me prisoner, as I should have done.
I, who was once their captive and their slave,
let the rain and the dog and the mountains intervene.
It is no longer enough to say – I will keep the roses for tomorrow.
The roses have need of me, and I them.
So, you will excuse me – if I leave you to your tomorrow.
I am taken prisoner by the roses.
And bid you, a sweet adieu.

All I Want

All I want, before the end
is a few days in the sun.
Somewhere to catch my breath.
That's all I ask.
Perhaps, an old apple tree –
and myself to sit there, with my head on your shoulder
and to tell you that I love you.
And to know that you love me.
A simple soul.
That's all I ask – before the end.

For Phil: written 26th June 2012 – and the sun IS shining.

Moments

Life is just a series of moments.
The moment when the two of you met.
The moment when you parted.
The moment when you thought
 you might just make it.
The moment when you almost gave up.
The moment when you soldiered on.
The moment when the lilac tree mam planted,
 flowered – first time ever.
The moment when storm clouds of the heart were gone.
The moment when all the unknown stories
 in the unknown books made sense.
The moment when the old dog died.
The moment when the new dog – just a puppy
 – stared at the empty space.
The moment when the kids opened their eyes.
The moment when they opened yours.
The moment that the sun became the moon.
The moment that your love was
 all that you could lean on.
The moment that you climbed the stairs,
threw your words into the dancing stars above
and knew that all was well
and sorrow, gone.
Life is just a limbo dance under the stars
of moments.

The Healing Pool

Yesterday was not a good day.
But, last night, I dreamed I was dipped in water.
In such a pool as I have never seen.
It was glorious – the water silver and deep
and luscious flowers growing all around.
And people balanced in the water, like acrobats
or dolphins, leaping higher as they gained strength.
(And I said, let me walk here forever.)
And around the edges of the pool were all manner
of creatures, living side by side – because over them
the waters had cast a spell. Of truth, of hope.
And two pools there were – and I was dipped in the first – then
    jumped myself, into the second
without a thought of harm or capture.
And the water washed over me, and was warm and rich on the body.
And seemed like an old friend.
And I wanted to stay and be beside this pool for ever.
Never to leave its warmth, its beauty.
And even now, I have no memory of leaving, or being asked to leave.
Only a voice saying 'Later my dear, later.'
And when I woke – sure, the world was turned around.

Different Snowdrops

Different snowdrops, different lives;
outside my window, a snowdrop is singing.
It is brave, so I am brave.
You say – let's go down to the woods
and see the snowdrops, the bluebells.
I don't even know where the woods are, except
the ones I've been living through all my life.
For you, the woods are just somewhere you visit
with picnic laughter and bright star feet.
For me, the woods are what I wake into each day

and try and crawl out of, make my way home.
But, just this snowdrop has come today – to say
one day, for you, there will be no more woods.
I could not explain this to you – how myself and this
white guardian sing out our hearts under the snow
that would bury us, crush us.
Just to stay alive. This is our aim.
And this cannot be explained.

Indigo

Maybe, one day,
in the lives between lives
(which lie like leaves or wounded soldiers)
they will bring me to a place of rest.
And they will bring Indigo to me – in a pot
of cool balm – and anoint me –
my head, my feet – and I will be whole, well again.
Maybe.
And, maybe they will say – rest little one
rest sister. For nothing can harm you now.
And you have done your best.

Maybe, one day,
in that place that I dream of
they will bring me to the ancient wells.
The wells of beauty and truth, of wisdom and grace.
And hope – which is the greatest of these.
And they will say – drink sister, drink dear child.
For there comes for you now, peace.
And under a golden tree by a river I will sit.
And count the golden apples that fall thereof.
And they will say – rest, for you have earned this place.
To you – we say welcome.
Of you, we are proud – rest child, rest sister.
For that other road is fading, on which you did your best.

Inside a Dog's Head

There are three words
inside a dog's head. Walk, friend and… sausages.

Throughout the day when they are not
devising a better philosophy for the world
these words run in tandem up and down
the field and in and out of the woods.
By the stream when they stop and give you that quizzical look
they are unlearning all that jeopardises and intimidates
happiness.

A dog always hopes that we will see sense and undo
all the harm we somehow inflict upon each other.
They explain the word friend while chasing their tails
or running for a stick.

But even while they spell it out
we walk back to the car, not seeing autumn under our feet
in need of scrunching. Not seeing the trees so fearful
of the white world that soon hangs on the branches.

But inside a dog's head – there will always be another spring.
Sausages for tea. And another friend to make.
Another walk to take – down to the silver stream.

(For Wendy and Pixie)

Dances With Dogs

My cousin it was, became known as
Dances With Dogs.
Always he denied it –
coming in from the pub and the old dog
sleeping on the hearth. But –
if the dog were to be believed – the dance it did
was true. Like a slow foxtrot or a samba –
on its hind legs.
Only after the whiskey –
if the whiskey had been avoided,
all was well. But, if not –
the dog would become Cinderella.
Hoofing round the small front room with
Johnny Cash playing, pretty loud.
Or Petula Clark – Downtown.
And to be fair – it had a natural grace and seemed
to take to the floor with ease.
But next day – there would be no mention of it.
just behind his back – ourselves –
twirling like spinning jennies
and barking and barking.
And him – catching our eye – turning sudden like.
Nothing like as nippy as the dog though.

The Sulking Dog

Does everything with a flounce.
He sighs – it is a huge chewed bone in the air.
He raises his eyes to the wood ceiling.
He will not come when called – he cocks a deaf un'.
He chews up clothes and fridge magnets.
He is spectacular in his expressions – they are
like a piano – a movement in dog major with
trumpet solo.
He sits with his back to you at the window.
He says his solicitor will be in touch about
the withholding of cookies.
We film him on camera when he is alone
trying out different poses of dejection and trying on
your mother's hat.
The sulking dog will come round in the end
and will forget what began it all.
But for now he shambles across to his basket
puts his arms over his head
and rings his therapist, Dr Bert.
Dr Bert advises rest. And muddy walks.
And cookies.
The sulking dog agrees.

Man Sweeping Leaves

So, it's like this.
A man is sweeping leaves in the garden.
He sweeps all the troubles of the world away.
I ask you what you are sweeping and you say
world peace into that corner
and against the flower border, an end to famine.
And in the centre, I say, where all the leaves are piled like
a mountain of souls?

That is all our happy days piled up together... lest we forget them.
And you sweep for another hour.
A man who understands the art of leaves
is a man amongst men.
And myself behind the glass reaching out to you,
to the air that swirls around you and speaks of an end to winter.
And the snowdrops by the door cheering you on.

Once I Knew

When I was a dancer, then
I knew what I was about.
I could pluck the blue sky and the moon
down from the sky and wear them both
and balance on the edge of clouds.
When I was a dancer.
When I was a dreamer, then
I knew what I was about.
I could hover over a green field and place
the heart of it into my ribs, and laugh
that I could do this.
When I was a dreamer.
When I was a sparrow, then
I knew what I was about.
I could tether the air to my wings
and become each tree, each drop of nectar
that dazzled me in flight.
When I was a sparrow.
When I was an apple, then
I knew what I was about.

Snowed In

And… some people spend their whole lives, snowed in.
But we've been lucky, we have braved the blizzard
and gotten soaked through to the skin.
Do you remember the funny house in Wales
and waking to a prisoner level of the white stuff.
It felt like a weight had been lifted from me.
I could just stay within the snow circle
and let the frost and the icicles do the rest.

Everything was white, my soul, my bones, my blood.
And yet I have never felt so alive.
As if a great drifting lay above and below me
and little particles of my small self dissolving
into the December day.
From the top window I could still see the world… just.
I could see the perfection of what might be achieved
if we could just hang on in there.
And a figure walking in the distance that I knew
to be myself.

The Poolside Babes

Are keen. Lean. Lean and mean, sometimes.
All think they are queen.
Out on the sunbeds at 9 o clock, then dipping
like oily fish in and out of the pool.
The water shimmers, they shimmer, no – glimmer –
and tremble like locusts in the heat.
Sunshine becomes them, they become sunshine.
The robust Americans, I marvel at them; the loose limbs,
the flowing hair. The German girls are more correct, less
trips to the bar, and they have a method in the pool.
A set routine.

The French girls are in wild bikinis, drink cocktails,
chatter loud as crickets and throw themselves like lunging
angels at the water.
The Swedes are casual, tall and perfect, steering into the blue
waters like longboats.
The Russian girls do not enter the water but sit on the edge and
keep a close eye on the elderly man they are with, his pacemaker,
his wallet.
The British girls are oiled with a frenzy by bored husbands,
(well, it's something to do)
and they must fetch the beer and the paper for him.
They all read *50 Shades of Grey*. And he nods off
dreaming of dusky maidens who wobble enticingly. Me?
I sit by the pool, near the dozing hammocks in my bandages
and cannot enter this oh so private heaven.
Sometimes they splash me on the way to the bar –
margaritas – a specialty of Spyros.
And for this smattering of life, I am grateful.

The Dogs of Corfu

We hear them barking in the night. All night.
You say they are not having a party.
In the day we pass the villas where they are chained,
or running free along the walls.
A little white one waits for us every night. She barks and barks.
Then three wild dogs set about your heels as we walk
down the last stretch home.
Two are huge, but the smaller one looks meanest.
Two large dogs behind a wall see them off,
and we almost run back to the hotel.
The only dogs we see in the day lie comfortable, asleep
outside tavernas where the smell of grilled chicken overpowers.
What cats we do see, look afraid and almost wilted in the heat.
Beware of the Dog is on every other gate, and I tell you
there is no crime on the island.
Wonder why?

Under the Old Tree, Corfu Town

Here we sit, and are happy.
Here, where the old lady goes through the bin,
where the old man sits next to us with the worry beads.
Where the thin grey cat eyes up your doughnut
with sudden magnolia eyes.
Where the café waitress with caramel skin and cookie dough arms
smiles across.
Where the elegant blonde lady walks her poodle.
Also elegant and happy.
Where the two Greek dancers (brothers) kick their heels
and slap their thighs and make the world more joyful.
Where the lemon tree shudders in the heat.
Where the fig tree sighs like a gentle breeze in the shade
and has the best of it.
Where the Jewish boy's sunglasses reflect the world in the
huge saucer mirrors.
Where a tray of melons is delivered, each bigger than the world.
Where you and I say – THIS then is the moment.
This is the moment to remember like a ripe kumquat
and this is the place to return to under this benevolent tree
that asks for nothing from us.
This is the place to return to, I say, when all is over, all is ended.
Just the scent of bougainvillea and gardenia
and you will find me my love.
Under this good-hearted tree and in no pain.
Rested and all is well.
You will find me.
You will find me.
You will find me.

A Certain Kind of Mist

Has arisen this morning over the field… and
it is blowing away our walk amongst the bluebells.
Sometimes mist takes… sometimes it gives.
Mist reaches out into the soul. Entwines itself there
like brambles on the open road… like a lost child…
like a star unknown on the way to being a comet.
On our bluebell walk there were hills and valleys
and a strange bright creature that walked with us.
It changed into a bird and then a tall rugged foxglove.
It had a story in its soul that was my own.
I said to you – how good it is to walk here
where my footsteps can echo the earth's heart once more.
And the bright creature smiled and shone the mist away.
And the mist she did not mind… and the song she sang
was the song of all good peoples as they walk
upon the earth, leaving only kind words and deeds.
That is the mist I dream of… hope to be
until the bluebell wood is come again, my love.

Picasso Woman

Today, again, I am her.
Picasso woman with all that that implies.
My nose is upside down and cabbage shaped,
my mouth suctioned to my breast
and my breast ramshackle in the hedgerow behind me.
My eye is in my foot, the other one throbs in my stomach
and keeps a close watch on the rest of me. My coiled hair
stretches from here to Timbuctoo and is both green and blue
and the eye in my stomach is lilac.
What's a gal to do?
My hands are nests of blackbirds coiled around the moon
and it's a privilege to wear these mermaid's legs.
The tail swishes and has its own buttonholed agenda
of summer days and mountain tops and misty nights and
eagle hearts. The eagle herself is my spine that never retreats.
My garden is full of the old boat that rocks, that I must call myself.
And the Picasso woman I am become smiles to see the pieces
I have become, without even trying.
I can paint myself no other ending than this, the whole of me
a curfew, a lighthouse, a word I did not know, a sparrow
sunning itself in the sun.

Glass Robins

As if they are.
Or is it me that is the glass bird in my silver cage,
unable to move
or fly.
They have built a temple to beauty and happiness in the
    elderflower bush
and I may sit and watch them.
They allow me in.
Their birds' wisdom is captivating.

Four of them, or maybe five, a lucky number
they fly so fast I cannot catch their eye
though they catch mine.
Glass in the wing, exquisite.
Bright and sharp and visible to God.
Emily Dickinson robins.
She had them in her mind's eye.
I have them, they have come to me for a reason
and I know it not.
Just that I am becoming glass, like a tiny mermaid or an
emperor butterfly crossing a bridge.
I will wield my red glass heart and send you all I can
of hope and feathers. I will be safe in the nest
for as long as I can be.
Then (the 6th bird) I will fly home.

Ballad of Penny Lane

I remember the first time
I heard Penny Lane.
We sang it at school, we sang it in the street
we sang it anywhere we could –
wherever young people meet.
I saved all me pocket money
to go to Liverpool to take the Ferry across the Mersey
and seek that lane out.
Everyone had their favourite Beatle.
Stuck the pictures of them from *Jackie* magazine
up on the bedroom wall.
They were what life in the Sixties
was all about.

Ringo's House

It's always the last one on the tour
and that's only if you ask – and then the driver
might, only might, go home that way.
No one knows much about it and they are
going to knock it down anyway.

Two women at the back say it's a scandal and ask
the man at the back with the dog called Clancey
what it looked like in its heyday –
What was the wallpaper like? The curtains?

But he can't remember – just that they were all in and out
of each other's houses all of the time.
Everybody was everyone's friend –
and that Ringo's mam did great fry-ups. And big mugs
of tea. And eggy bread.

And it's getting really dark now – because John and Paul's houses
    took such a long time
and it's the whole street in twilight, a kind of purple twilight
    suitable for a drummer
as we all sit quiet as if we were at mass, and look the house
up and down as if we were buying some song from the past.

And the man with the dog gets out for a smoke –
and another car pulls up – and asks the way to George's house.
And the house of the drummer that will soon be ashes
that will soon be just dust gives out a long sigh
into the Liverpool night.

And through the window you can see that the wallpaper
is green and still intact and that across one of
the boarded-up bits – someone has written LOVE ME DO.
'It's a damn shame,' says the chunkiest of the women
and hands round cheese sandwiches while
the other one gets out and leans against the wall like
a Da Vinci figure – and puts her hand up against the window.

And one by one we all get out – and sure enough the driver
starts to sing *Love Me Do* – and the dog barks along.
And suddenly it's 1963 again – and the Cavern is
just down the road. And all of us are young.
And the house glows in the twilight.
And everything still to play for – hope in our hearts
in the compelling and deafening Liverpool night.

The Trees at the Cemetery

In their defence I will say this.
They see us, even though we do not see them.
We trudge with our watering cans and lilies
and our memories
– and we see and understand nothing.
We do not see their strange and living shapes –
how they move and dart in the wind.
How they are undefeated by the stars.
Their sweet and pleasant journey in the air.
We are prisoners of a different vision. We climb a
different mountain. We do not hear the melody,
that rich and haunting tune.
But they see us. Hear us.
We look – and look away. Such fools we are.
Even when they keep the sky from falling on our heads
we do not see though the long grass, how they keep
our feet from falling.
No.
Only the shadows that are visible we see, as damaged
and unmendable, they fall across our path.
The deep roots that cross from grave to grave,
that almost could derail us.
This is what we see.
When we leave,
we do not see the arms around that wave,
nor the green richness,
the driving beauty of this meadow.
We do not hear the song of hope
that always they gather in –
nor with each spring how gladly they return –
are Kings and Queens of blossom.
We do not see them.
But, always, they see us.

Flowers by the Roadside

As if to mask death a bunch of dahlias
is pinned to a tree.
They look like another accident
they look like a murmured apology
a dedication to the person who put them there.
Small children gather and parents put
tulips in their hands.
This could be the wrong place.
This is the wrong place.
Snails, rabbits, birds chew and grizzle
at the so-called tokens.
This is a white world full of nothing
and no one's thoughts.
This is borrowed death growing by the minute
a limbo of meaningless crap
the kids do not understand,
but they know more than the parents.
There are no victims
we are all running in our own race.
Can you name the bullet, can you name the spot?
Nothing too bad happens if you hear Vivaldi.
The Easter bunny drips chocolate onto
little Mary's arm
'What is death Mama, what is death Papa?'
A rose by any other name should not be left here.

Climbing Trees

Soft as tissue paper the tree smiles.
Phil tells me how many trees he's climbed.
Me, I've never climbed a tree
and that is what my life lacks.
I am all hugging trees but he is climbing the tree,
scaling and ascending up up into the blue air –
why is the air always blue? Probably isn't, you know –
up into the Turneresque air.
Now look how I try to make a poem of it
but Phil has simply climbed the tree
and this is what my life lacks.
I would like him to climb more trees in our front room.
We must install more, and we do today
a rowan, an oak and an ash
a willow, the willow tree is special
the nearest I ever got to climbing a tree
and this is what my life has lacked.
In the dream my hands and arms work again.
I cheer, I laugh to see my beautiful hands again
beauty is in the eye of the beholder.
I have never held a bee, I have never climbed a tree
and this is what my life has lacked.
And Phil is tall as a tree
and stretches up up into the atmosphere
as if he is flying a kite
as if he is in Mary Poppins
as if he is a magical hare
as if he is a fox climbing a tree
at the top of the tree will be white sliced bread
toasted like on an old galley train
and we will climb and climb
and the tree will be wonderful.

What we build in the tree, soft wonderful tree,
the things you can hide in the tree
and this is what my life has lacked.
The tree is Monroe, the tree is an eagle
the tree is a rowan, all singing all dancing
and still Phil climbs
and he reaches a hand down to me
gives me a hand up and I follow him up the tree
the tree beyond words of beauty
the tree that I have lacked, he gives me back,
he gives me back
that tree that tree he gives me back so many trees
I lose count of them
and himself walking in a forest
not caring but always daring
a magician tree, a Phil tree
my tree of always
and now I finally get to climb that tree.

If I had never seen a butterfly

The world would be broken and smaller
my one, only flight would be baffled and weary
my own wings hanging unused
my own soul held under water by a dark stone
the scent of jasmine gone from my hair
the wild lilac no longer adrift
the crushed butterfly at my parents' grave
a mystery of remembered truth
a bell that does not sound
a cloud whose name is freedom
left to languish in my heart
a burden begun when there was none
a mountain top and no way to ascend
a lover's picture speaks to myself
but the language and the words undone
if I had never seen the butterfly
what reason to say the brutal act of wisdom
that greets tomorrow
as if I were a bird of wonder
of innocence, of captured joy
if I had never seen the butterfly
I would with my whole heart
invent

The Valley of Happy Songs

The valley of happy songs is where I want to live.
The valley of happy songs is all that Wales can give
when the midnight curlew sings
when the sloeberry blossoms.
The valley of happy songs is drifting and a dreaming.
The valley of happy songs is where I want to live.
The valley of happy songs is a cadence
that I have never heard before.

The valley of happy songs overwhelms, overcomes me.
The valley of happy songs is where I'll walk one day with you my love.
The valley of happy songs is in my heart and in my head.
The valley of happy songs is where I'll walk one day.
The valley of happy songs is beautiful, so beautiful I cannot tell you.
The songs you sing there you've never heard before,
the songs that were sung there were with you when you were born
will be with you when you leave.
The valley of happy songs is where I'll walk one day.

New Childhood

In this our new religion
you feed me, clothe me, bathe me
and when people come and ask how we are
we smile and say, we are fine and dandy, doing good.
And our hearts beat a little faster at the mask we wear.
A mask is not new to us
and we are adept at wearing.
Like a shell at the sea's edge, I lean on you and you on me.
The birds of the air pull us through another day.
The song of the ocean is you
and I am a small sparrow diving into the midnight hours of morning.
Outside my window a blackbird asks how we are
and him we can tell.
You pour me a glass of wine,
it is the colour of fine roses
and we drift and dream into the heart of it.
We sew each other back together
watch *Rebel Without A Cause*
and thank our lucky lucky stars
that the moon has been ours to take as lover… one more time.

Leaving Messages in Trees

As a child, a fanciful child – (still am)
I used to leave messages in trees.
And with the message, a small acorn and perhaps
a flower. A sprig of blossom, a forget-me-not.
The tallest tree – a big old oak on Low Moor –
a real battler – always had the most to say.
I used to leave the best message there – because I thought
this wise old self held most of the answers.
(Seeking answers, even then.)
Mam would help me place it there, and wait further down
the hill while I said my tree prayer.
But trees know better than to give response – only the sky
above them and the roots below the sky will they speak of.
And this is as it should be.
'The skies, roots and the bird that lives in the moon – they
sing. Let this be our answer to you.
Now away with you.'
Only once – a piece of paper (Mam's writing) 'I Love You'.
And this the answer that I treasure.
And this the answer that I keep.

NOTES

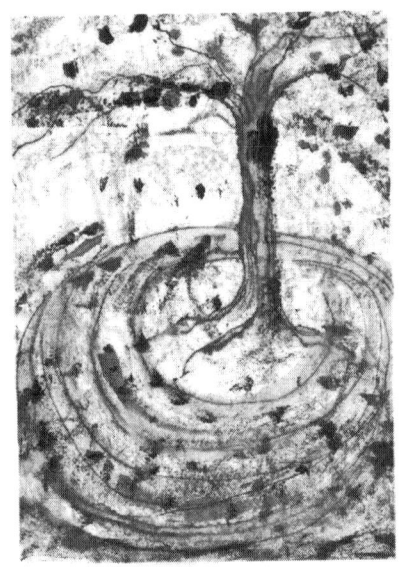

— from the garden (1969) —

Love is the Feeling Between Now and Now (p.17)
The Skyline / The Lens of the Camera (p.18)

I wrote these poems – my first ever! – after a friend brought round a book of Dylan Thomas. I was utterly amazed that anyone could write like that; I had an almost physical reaction, and wrote twenty poems in a single day. I sent Jamie scans of the notebook, and he chose these three, as they apparently sounded the most finished and made the most sense.

— from *A Game of Two Halves* (1979) —

Welcome (p.19) – This is a short poem written while I was talking to some friends who are peace campaigners. I had become very interested in why we say what we say and do what we do. In the fullness of time all that people remember is how it made them feel.

Piano (p.19) – This poem was set to music and performed in Australia. I was delighted at this. I wanted it to be an exploration of the night, but simply and delicately like music. The man who devised the music was a Quaker called Tony, who had a stroke in my house but was found just in time.

Heart (p.20) – This is a poem written in memory of a very dear friend who had just died of a heart attack. He was a lovely man and I was very sad for many years after his death. He planted some forget-me-nots at the back door that bloomed and bloomed.

Poem for Mrs Waters (p.21) – This poem won a prize in a Jersey Poetry competition. It is about a lady who lived next to my Aunty Kath. She was the official 'layer-outer' of the area. She was a small, chatty lady and I liked her a lot. I remember she wore smart cardigans and beautiful beads and had the thickest glasses you ever saw.

Batsi, Andros (p.22) – This is about the island of Andros, which I visited with a friend whose nickname was Pixie. This was the first time he had visited Greece and he loved it. He bought me a Greek key design necklace in Batsi. This poem was read at his funeral after he died of a heart attack.

Foreigner (p.23) – This was about someone I went to Turkey with and how even after so many years you can still not really know a person. A case of two people being too alike? Being two Scorpios we argued on and off for fifteen years. I won!

In May (p.24) – This poem was about a dear friend called Bob who died in May, very suddenly of a heart attack. I like to think he would have liked the poem. He was a remarkable and gentle soul and his death was a huge loss to so many people.

Lacing Boots (p.25) – This poem was written at Beamish and is about some boots my friend Jacky and I bought in 1969. They were very hip, the best boots I ever had, so cool. They represented happiness and freedom. We wore them till they were through. I think Twiggy and Julie Driscoll had a pair. What finer provenance!

The Film (p.26) – I went for an audition for a film while I worked in Birmingham. I didn't get it as my hair was too long to go under the wig but it was a fun experience. I think the film was a period piece, so perhaps not for me.

The Aunts (p.28) – This is about the two Irish aunts, Sarah and Lella, who brought my dad up after his parents died. They were both potato pickers and they were both extraordinary women. Sarah was tough and practical. Lella, short for Mary Ellen, was more fey and fond of reciting poetry. Because where I live isn't far from their house, I often feel there is a certain continuity to life and to their stories. This poem won the Suffolk Poetry Prize, judged by Anthony Thwaite. It was also published in *The Rialto*.

Windmills (p.29) – This is about a friend of mine called Scilla who I went to philosophy classes with, and another friend called Gwen who I still see and sometimes sing David Bowie with. It is about being a free spirit.

Sun (p.30) – This poem is after a very close friend who died and my attempt to see the positive side and stay on the bright side of the road.

The Prepared Room (p.31) – I wanted to explore the concept of dying and other forms of existence … cheerful little soul aren't I?

At Highfield (p.32) – This poem is about a hospital I went to in Droitwich Spa for my arthritis. It was the old style of Spa hospital, very friendly, a home from home, if you will. Very happy memories of the hydrotherapy pool there, and the food was great – you actually had a choice. The garden was exquisite and I honed my Brummie accent to perfection there. They used to put Emmerdale on to make me feel at home, not knowing I detest it!

At Elvington (p.33) – This is for my friend, Pix, who died. I had a gravestone made with a Wallace Stevens quote on it: "When the blackbird flew out of sight, / It marked the edge / Of one of many circles." It is from 'Thirteen Ways of Looking at a Blackbird'. Pix was from Elvington; a lovely village near York.

— from *Leros: Island of Dreams* (1994) —

Arrival – Leros (p.34) – This is the lead poem from my book of poetry written about Greece. I went on a walking holiday there with a group of orchid hunters. It ended spookily for me as everyone else went home and I was left on my own at an isolated villa.

Here – Now (p.34) – This is me trying to be a bit painterly and spontaneous about Greece – but it's impossible to capture Greece in any way – like trying to pin down smoke. The colours and the light have to be lived through.

Wing (p.35) – This poem explores Greece from a birdlike point of view – with me as the bird. The wounded bird wondering what flight really means. I went to Greece for three weeks as part of a walking tour to look for a very rare orchid on the island of Leros.

Ankle-Deep (p.36) – This is about suffering from spondylitis. The leader of the orchid troupe also had it, so we shared our experiences – his had been very different as he was from a wealthy background. Money and bad health is a superior cocktail to a lack of money and bad health!

Swallows at Aghia (p.37) – This poem was written outside the belt shop on Leros. I love swallows and was moved by their home-building antics. I wanted to be one of them.

Aghia Marina (p.38) – This is about the impossible beauty of Greece. I am outside the belt shop again. I aim to be a bit surreal here, a bit like a conjuror's image of Greece.

Alinda Bay (p.39) – This is about one of the girls who make themselves available on the island. I tried to explore this in a different way, without being a hypocrite or numpty.

At the Castle (p.40) – This is about climbing the hill with a rather strange lady called Jean. She was a troubled soul and struck up a friendship with me. Looking back I can see just how traumatised she was. Probably a closet poet …

V.E. Day (p.41) – I wanted to acknowledge the debt we owe.

Dawn (p.41) – This is a simple poem – sometimes words get in the way of truth. Less will do it better.

The Traveller (p.42) – This has become a popular poem over the years. The traveller is an almost Bob Dylan gypsy-esque figure. Who they are is of no consequence, it's how you perceive and remember them.

Villa (p.43) – This is the place I stayed at, a beautiful villa that seemed to have an unusual ambience. Left on my own there it became a bit spooky, and someone tried the handle of my door one night. I was terrified!

Saint George's Chapel (p.44) – This was a place I felt deserved a mention. It's not on Leros – I found it exploring Crete some years earlier. Very lovely.

For Bob (in Leros) (p.44) – This was written for Bob as a keepsake. The oxalis is a good symbol for him, a wild daisy, perfect and generous. The language of flowers is often so apt to describe people.

At Garbo's (p.45) – This is about a restaurant I went to on Leros with a group of fellow travellers. We were a bunch of mixed souls, all on our own, and we adopted this restaurant for three weeks. The owners were fun and very jolly. I think they were from London and so welcoming to us all. I remember an Irish man called John telling lots of stories.

Patmos (p.46) – This is a fun piece about Saint John. The only way to take faith is with a side salad of humour – for me anyway.

Papa Retsina (p.46) – This is about the laid back priest on the island. He was very popular!

Leros Cat-Walk (p.47) – There are always so many cats on Greek islands that they had to have their own poem. It is true about dreams on Leros, they are often shared – rather Jungian and freaky.

Vortex (p.48) – This poem is about the strange fact that people on Leros often dream the same dream.

Departure (p.48) – This is a very simple poem, partly inspired by a John Martyn song, which celebrates roses.

Kallinichta (p.49) – This means 'good night' in Greek and was written on my last night on Leros. I was trying to capture the beauty of Greece.

— from *Poetry* (1995) —

Tigers (p.50) – This poem was written at a writing workshop run by a very young Simon Armitage in the seventies! I remember he particularly liked the line: 'without permission, everything is possible.' It was one of those poems that seems to come out of nowhere – I have read it as a finale piece at many readings over the years. It has become a bit of a credo.

New Girl at the Shop (p.51) – I once worked at Boyes in York. I was an appalling shop girl and actually got a man's trousers caught in the till while selling an Easter egg.

Map (p.52) – This I dedicate to all men and their usage of maps. Not that I'm much better!

Fireworks (p.54) – This was about my partner at that time, Duncan, who always enjoyed making fires, much to people's amusement. We were in Wales at the time.

Space (p.55) – A young poem written about relationships that break up ... strange when you look back, how unimportant these things now seem.

Walkers (p.56) – This is about two young boys called Robert and Andrew walking in Wales in 1993. They were Bob's sons and we were on holiday in mid Wales.

The Op (p.57) – This is about the hip operations I had in Birmingham. Both hips were replaced and I had to stay in bed for three months. I learnt how to eat cornflakes lying down.

Sheep (p.58) – This is an early-ish poem. I was visiting Wales a lot at the time. I really do think sheep are party animals on the quiet.

Fever Flowers (p.59) – This is about a little girl that my friend Heather knew. I like the concept of fever, it has a feeling all its own I think.

The Flying Suit (p.60) – This is about what happens after relationships break up, and the extremes of feeling we put ourselves through. As I am a person of extremes this was easy to write. I have lived my life always in the grip of some extreme or other.

George (p.61) – This poem is about a strange chap who used to call in at the jobcentre where I worked, every day. He was eccentric to say the least.

Oz (p.62) – This is about a young man I knew who went to Australia. He went out there to be a nurse in Sydney and really loved it. He died very young in his early fifties.

Leaving (p.63) – This is about the concept of leaving, shuffling off this mortal coil. What does leaving actually mean? What does it mean to remain?

Another Song (p.64) – This is about working class heroes. My dad dug and laid many of the roads in the city of York, and it was a certain type of lifestyle for a man who really should have been on the stage as a song and dance man. The idea of a different song to sing always moves me ... it occurs in the film *Educating Rita*. I once shared an ashtray with Willy Russell in Ilkley. Claim to fame! My dad worked with an interesting bunch of men, mainly Irish. 'Danny Boy' was my dad's favourite song and it was sung at his funeral. This poem was published in a Hull anthology and was also read at Hull Literature Festival accompanied by the musician Simon Davey playing 'Danny Boy'.

Aldeburgh (p.65) – This is me recalling time spent there with my friend Bob. I remember him picking up shells there. He was a dear and gentle soul and we shared a sense of humour.

On Coats (p.66) – This is about helping my mum at the catholic jumble sales. It was a treat to be able to help her – I felt so proud and important doing this. Some of my happiest memories were there, down at the church hall where mam was in sole charge of coats.

Whale (p.68) – This is about discussing whales with my dad, we often had strange philosophical conversations. This one was a conversation about what a whale's dream must be like. He also told me once he thought he had been a sculptor in a former life and that when he was dead he would simply be a piece of paper blowing in the wind. He was an enigma wrapped in fish and chip paper and mam was a mystery to both of us. This poem went on to win the York Poetry Competition judged by Ian McMillan.

— from *Midnight in the Morning* (1998) —

Hope Street (p.69) – This is about the Hope Street round the corner from me. The Irish in York always got a raw deal but were always a wondrous part of the city.

Therapy (p.70) – This is about all the different and often pretentious new age therapies I was into in the nineties. I went on so many courses and these references are very true. Especially the reference to Merthyr!

Mellow Yellow (p.72) – This is a crazy poem about different guys I knew in the sixties, an amalgamation, if you will. All of these facts are real! Especially the guy eating the banana!

Foxglove (p.73) – Foxgloves are a flower I have always loved, and it was a pleasure to imagine myself as a foxglove. This poem won a prize in the Norwich poetry competition. I also won the first prize that year with another poem! The man judging it was amazed when he realised both poems were by me. (See 'Gargunnock', p.79.)

Snake (p.74) – I always wanted to like snakes, but never can somehow. I think it's the shedding of the skin which reminds me of myself. I finally saw a snake up close in India. It was being charmed – or was it charming?

India (p.75) – This was written after a trip to Goa with some friends. What an extraordinary country and how I wish I could go back there now. The people are a delight and it was a fantastic experience, happy memories.

The City (p.76) – This poem was written at an Arvon centre in Devon. It was imagining a perfect city where all is peace and all is well. The city of lanterns is also a street in Chicago and a festival in Truro.

Sea-Largo (p.77) – Sea-Largo represents the sea as it relates to myself and my mum – she was only really happy by the sea. I wanted to capture that feeling of complete joy in this poem. I am only lately come to the sea. As a painter I understand it better than as a poet. I think it does not like to converse, but prefers just to be. This poem was published in *Dream Catcher* magazine.

Irish Funeral (p.78) – This is about a funeral I went to at St. Wilfrid's Church in York with my dad, one of his old drinking cronies had died. The Irish have a way with death. I think it makes them doubly alive.

Gargunnock (p.79) – This poem won first prize in the Norwich poetry competition, the same year 'Foxglove' won. It was written at a house near Stirling called Gargunnock where I went to a murder mystery weekend. Very beautiful, but the weather was appalling.

Boatman (p.80) – This is about an imagined and mysterious boatman. A bit like a character out of a John Fowles novel, you are not sure what they represent or where they come from. They take you by surprise and, like the ferryman, require some form of payment. May not be what you want to give …

— from *The Book of Beyond* (2001) —

Recipe for a Poet (p.81) – This is about how one might construct a poet. A little more assonance and a touch of the vernacular, then the eyes of Emily Dickinson and the mouth of Rumi … just a thought!

The Happening (p.83) – This is me being surreal, just for a change, about the nature of events – are they even real? Are we real, does an event come before us or after? You could say I was born enquiring.

Billy (p.85) – This is about a miserable guy who looked after the gates to the local cemetery. People cheered when he left. Went to live in Halifax … God help Halifax.

Second-hand Men (p.86) – This was always a popular poem at readings. This was me remembering loads of chaps I had met over the years. I merge them here, I must write 'second-hand women' one of these days.

Home Town (p.87) – This won the Devon and Dorset poetry competition. It was about a young lad that my partner knew from football matches. His life was quite poignant – that struggle to leave somewhere, but being tied to a place with nowhere else to go.

Lazarus Enrolls at the Gym (p.88) – I have always enjoyed taking the Michael out of the so-called serious stuff. I hope both Michael and Lazarus would be proud here.

The Back of Beyond (p.90) – This must be a real place I figure. Like Timbuctoo, I would so like to go there. But just to visit, I like to live more in the hub myself.

The Test (p.91) – This is my father's biggest disappointment in life, not having a car.

Enlightenment (p.92) – Again, this is a wild-eyed look at the truth that lies out there just waiting to be uncovered. I plan to be the one to do it. My chances I would say are 50/50.

Timothy (p.93) – This is a poem Phil has always really liked and, like so many others, he gave me the idea for. We still refer to Timothy to this day, he never phones … he never writes …

Town People on a Beach (p.95) – As I am an inveterate townie, this is me and Phil being very nervous on a beach. Unfamiliar territory always worries me. I need a little help out of the maze that is the world.

Silver Wedding (p.96) – There's sarky, now.

Good Advice (p.97) – This is something I have never heeded. Like the character in *Withnail and I*, I have gone on holiday by mistake. It's only looking back that I can see what fun it's been. Whether or not you heed advice people still give it, it's made of puppy-dog's-tails a lot of the time but you never can tell.

Neil, Honey (p.98) – We always remember where we were when they landed on the moon. And when they shot Kennedy. I remember dad went to bed and me and mam sat up and saw it all.

Making Ends Meet (p.99) – This is a topical poem, exploring the issues of how we meet people.

The Dog in the Painting (p.100) – This is about imagining myself to be a dog and all that this real or unreal existence has to offer. I would have liked to have owned a dog called Zorro.

Sundays (p.101) – This is one of Phil's favourite poems. It was almost a prose poem I think, and encapsulates a Catholic childhood.

Message (p.102) – This is about a flatmate I had in Newcastle, the joys of flat-sharing are many and various. Most of these things actually happened. Happy days. I am still very fond of Newcastle and start speaking Geordie when I am stressed.

— from *Zuzu's Petals* (2007) —

The Chocolate Girls (p.103) – York is a city based on chocolate and this poem is about all the amazing people that worked at Terry's and Rowntrees – trying to encapsulate their very essence, if you like. This poem has been part of a live theatre show for International Women's Week – and is also used by people who visit care homes to remind the residents of their younger days.

Children's Games (p.104) – This was one of my favourite poems ever; it won the Yorkshire poetry prize one year and has been performed a million times. I like it because it contains so many memories and it is me running amok with them. I think I am still a child in many ways. It is an unusual poem in that it has a repeat rhythm – and almost a kind of lyric feel to it. All the games mentioned in the poem, I played as a kid – these were an only child's games, an Anglo-Irish child's games – Catholic and wild and obsessive.

When Dad was Father Christmas (p.106) – This is about my dad being Father Christmas at Fenwick department store in York for many years. It was the job he always dreamed of doing, and he was super at it, he intrigued the kids and they him. I think he liked the non judgemental nature of kids coming to see Santa. He took to wandering York in the costume quite illegally.

The Apple House (p.108) – This was written down in Woodbridge in Suffolk, what inspired it I am not sure. I was visiting my friend Martin Crix at the time. I like the idea of being an apple and our house in York was built on an orchard.

Head (p.110) – This was written about my mum, who was not well for many years. So many ladies seem to suffer from a funny head. My mum's was more serious than that – she bore all of it like a victorious queen.

Strange Meeting (p.112) – This was about two identical twins that lived near me as a kid. They dressed in old fashioned clothes and had their own language. This poem was published by York St. John's University in their student magazine while I was studying a Literature M.A. there.

The Space Around (p.113) – I played around with lots of rhythms and rhymes in this poem. It was inspired by the idea of negative space in painting. Everything coexists in space in a way. Even us ...

The Blue Cooker (p.114) – This was a fun piece inspired by my own very old cooker at Melbourne Street. It won the Southport comedy prize. My cooker was green but was equally temperamental. My dad was the kiss of death to cookers and once, when he cooked an Irish stew, the pan had to be clinically disposed of.

Children's Hospice (p.116) – This was written about a hospice in York called St Leonard's, of which people speak very highly. The children seem very real, not ghosts at all.

The York Floods (p.117) – A poem about when the city flooded badly and we took a walk to see it all.

Be Careful (p.118) – This is an incident from when I was about seven or eight and my dad was laying new tiles in our kitchen. He was about as good a handyman as Frank Spencer (from *Some Mothers Do 'Ave 'Em*) and the whole scenario was a nightmare. It was very frightening as a child to see my mum weeping with the distress of it all.

Tortoises (p.119) – This is about all the rubbish that gets put through your door. May as well be tortoises? This is still a Phil and I joke to this day. We totally share a sense of humour.

The Point of Men (p.120) – This is self explanatory, and although I get on best with men not women, I wanted to say this to show I can see what happens ... The men in my life have been my lucky talisman.

Full Fruit Salad (p.120) – This is a bit of fun. A lady very sheepishly bought a print of this poem from me once, while checking all round to see she wasn't observed!

Dear Rucksack (p.121) – This is about the various travels of my rucksack. I love that rucksack and wish I still had it. Must check the loft!

In My Day (p.122) – A poem about when my dad was in hospital during the last month of his life. We argued constantly but I loved him to bits. He was an enigma wrapped in a bottle of Guinness – if you thought you had an answer from him he would promptly change the question.

Donor (p.122) – This is just me being an old hippy and wishing for world peace. And so I always will.

How to Spot a Poet (p.123) – This poem is asking 'what is this whole poetry lark about?' After 45 years I'll be damned if I know. Answers on a postcard. "I've become a poet by mistake." À la *Withnail and I*.

The Other House (p.124) – This is about the massive long battle with ill health I have had. You have to believe there is more to it, to survive.

— from *The Ruby Slippers* (2011) —

Quiet Auditorium (p.125) – This was one of the first poems I ever had published. It won a prize and a place in an anthology of poetry judged by the poet Vernon Scannell, launched at Ilkley Literature Festival. It was also one of the first poems I wrote after returning to live in Yorkshire from Birmingham. I moved to a house that dated from the 1600s, a house that seemed to have many 'ghosts'. I would almost say they wrote the poem.

On Wearing My Uncle Patrick's Hat (p.126) – This was a poem written about my Uncle Pa, who died when I was eight – he was 88.

He was a very quick-witted man, who served in the Boer War, and was usually a winner in the Whit Walks in the city. I wrote the poem while wearing his trilby hat bought at the local co-op in the 1930s (it cost 2 and 6, I believe). The poem has now been translated into Romanian – also read on Romanian (BBC) radio, and featured in an Anglo-Romanian anthology and CD.

The Grenz (p.127) – This was a poem about a real incident that happened to my dad when he was serving in the Second World War. Under cover of darkness he smuggled some refugees to safety. The poem won the Manchester International Poetry Prize in 1996 and was read at the prize giving there. This was the first poem I ever read in public, at Nellie's Bar in Beverley.

The Dancing Room (p.128) – Before I got arthritis, I did ballet dancing for many years in York. It was my big passion in life – I did several stage shows and hoped to make dancing my career. I try to dance with words now – and wanted to capture my lost world in this poem. This poem was commended in the William Soutar House Competition.

My Red Sandals (p.130) – I didn't have Ruby Slippers as a child – but I did have an amazing pair of red sandals – which I loved! In the poem they represent innocence, timelessness – childhood itself, almost.

Racing Caterpillars (p.132) – It was written as a fun piece about the caterpillars in matchboxes that my cousin Catherine and I used to race at my Aunty Mary's house. I never had a pet – these were the nearest I ever got to one! Other pets were too expensive.

The Gift (p.133) – This poem was the 'title track' of the CD I brought out in 2000. It is the one poem on the CD I struggled to read because it is about my mum, who was an incredibly strong character. The boxes referred to in the poem contained her wedding ring and her engagement ring. She gave them to me when she knew she was quite ill; they are the only gold I have. I still wear them. She was a very private woman and this was a very special moment with her.

Bless This Handbag (p.134) – This is about my mother's handbag, which went everywhere with her. It was a kind of talisman and a standing joke between us that I never liked it, because it didn't go with anything. It is quite true that she often had rice pudding or chicken soup in it, just in case of an emergency. She did not regard herself as an eccentric just very practical. I still have the bag in our book room.

Avoiding Stories (p.136) – This was written much later than the preceding poems, while I was living back in the city and trying to do lots of different courses and workshops – trying things on for size, if you will. My life was a bit chaotic at this time. This is after a most peculiar week when lots of silly things happened. I have garnered them together and added a few silly garnishes which I trust are entertaining.

Sandra is a Child of Peace and Love (p.138) – This poem was published in an anthology of material from a stage show I did for about two years. The show was called 'Subterranean Homesick Yorkshire Blues' and toured several festivals and theatres. 'Sandra' in the poem was a girl I knew in the sixties/early seventies when I was a student in Newcastle. The Knebworth concerts were a pilgrimage for us – they were very happy days.

Why I Fancy Him (p.140) – This is about my partner Phil, he is my world and my delight. He is the reason I am still here. We like the same words and have the same thoughts, it's like cosmic engineering – only better. When one glove is lost, both are lost and that would be true of us. He has the sexiest of everything, which I still feel every time I see him.

The Ruby Slippers (p.141) – It is a true story of shoe-shopping in a wheelchair – a task I do not recommend to you, on any level. Those Ruby Slippers are the only ones for me, and – like Cinderella's glass one – they seem to fit me perfectly. All of this is true, we were happy before we went into the shop … I have the most beautiful shoes which my damaged feet cannot wear. Heaven will be full of shoes and chocolate.

The Green Field (p.143) – Originally published in *Dream Catcher* magazine. 'The Green Field' is also now a children's story I am writing; it has come to symbolise the fruition of everything I have tried to aim for in life. I suppose it is an idyllic place – an Ithaca I hope to reach one day. Here's hoping.

Owls (p.144) – Originally a performance piece at the Suffolk Poets 'Schubertiad' in 2010. This was a Viennese-inspired evening and the poem was followed by wonderful piano music by Holger Aston. It was written down by the river in York one Saturday. I am especially fond of owls, as was Phil's aunt Doreen. I often imagine her to be an owl that looks after us when she can. She smoked too much and was great fun to be with. Good on yer Doreen. These owls are mysterious and hard to work out.

At the Foreigners' Club (p.145) – I have visited Sorrento several times now, and would say Italy is my favourite country – the Foreigners' Club is an extraordinary place with a view across Sorrento Bay that is incredible. I hope the poem captures something of the joy and exuberance of the Italian people.

On the 14th Deck of the Cruise Ship Aurora (p.146) – This poem was written while travelling to the Baltic on a cruise ship. There is no fourteenth deck on the ship concerned – but this was my imagining of what might be up there. There is a certain etiquette to cruise ships which is very entertaining.

The Rehabilitation Hobbies Room (p.147) – This poem won second prize in the Ver Poets Open Competition in 2010. It was inspired by my own experience, on the road to recovery after numerous leg operations. It is culled from a lot of my hospital wanderings, and takes the Mickey I hope – that is really all you can do with bad health, and I believe it deserves nothing more.

Stay in Touch (p.148) – This poem was first published as part of a small origami booklet printed and distributed in Rhode Island by the Origami Poets, Jan Keough and Lynne Gobeille, whose inspirational brainchild this whole project was. This poem is in my first booklet with them and it's inspired by that classic old phrase.

Drawing Dogs (p.149) – This poem was the lead poem of my third booklet with the Origami Poets. Dogs always stay in touch because they are honest and compassionate and have no boundaries. I do a lot of artwork now, and dogs are some of my favourite images to draw. Especially Wendy, Pixie and Molly dog. We love all of you.

The Shape of Hands (p.150) – This poem about my mother was published in *The Rialto*. It is that strange sense of seeing a person who is no longer here, through your own image. Hands, I feel, are a very evocative image. It is a quiet introspective piece about what we inherit ... my mother was very proud of her hands and I was also asked to be a hand model.

Tomorrow (p.151) – This poem, like the much earlier one, 'Tigers', has become a major poem for me – it makes a statement of how I hope life could one day be. That sense of waiting for tomorrow is crucial to me as I have had arthritis now for forty years. So, tomorrow for me, is when that will end. It is me wishing for the moon to descend into the world.

The Road Out of Town (p.152) – I wrote this poem especially for publication of *The Ruby Slippers*, to bring an end to all these landmark steps as I've travelled my own 'Yellow Brick Road.' Maybe, when I get to the Emerald City, I will find out what it has all been about. It has been a hurricane – and Kansas is still a very long way off – but like Ithaca, what the journey and the poems have given me has, I believe, been worth it. It is me musing on the road that will finally be taken. It's a bit American and Irish in feel, with a hint of Welsh ... What most of my poems embody I suppose. My mum used to say I write in Irish, but I think an American voice supersedes this now. America is my birthplace and Paris my hometown? Corny huh?! Someone has to be.

— from *And God Said Let There Be Chocolate* (2013) —

And God Said Let There Be Chocolate (p.153) – This is me celebrating my favouritist thing in life ... chocolate. I think if you have lived in York, home of Nestle and Terry's, chocolate is in your DNA. This poem was inspired on a cold rainy day in February – trying to make believe that Spring is about to arrive. I wanted it to be life affirming – and I hope it achieves that.

Chocolate Credo (p.154) – Again a celebration of chocolate, I put together a book of chocolate poems and people always seem to enjoy them. Apparently dark chocolate affects the brain differently and is the hard core substance of chocolate lovers. Milk chocolate is very much trailer trash ... This was specifically written when I heard there was to be a York Chocolate Festival. I have always believed in the power of chocolate and I hope I always will.

The Refuseniks (p.155) – This poem reflects a period of time when I was working in Birmingham – and at that time, so many of my work colleagues were on diets it seemed almost a crime to speak of chocolate. As it was prohibited to them – it was, of course, what they craved the most. I think there should be much more 'yes' in life than 'no'.

The Little Chocolate Soldier (p.156) – This is me I think. What am I trying to prove with my toy story games? Can you win or lose by how you walk through the fire? By how you become a warrior? This is a seemingly innocent poem – but I hope it reflects something a little deeper, about the nature of people and the world.

In Which Dad is 'Dances With Chocolate' (p.157) – This is a fair description of my home life. Dad was a huge chocolate fan, though mam preferred a nice mint Imperial. Dad and I had our own drawers for chocolate and woe betide if any went astray. My Uncle Pat had a separate drawer for Caramac. It's the little things I remember. This is a fun piece and brings back many happy memories of my childhood; my mother and father were huge influences on my world and my writing.

The Creature from the Chocolate Lagoon (p.158) – This is a fun piece, dedicated to the girls who work at the chocolate factories in the city. I have tried to embody it as best I could. There are so many moods to chocolate it is easy to run amok with them sometimes. I wanted to imagine that there might actually be a kind of animal living in the chocolate. A kind of Viking version of Sooty perhaps! And of course, it should be taken to a good home.

The Smarties Room (p.159) – This is where my dad used to work when he worked at Rowntrees and later Terry's. He used to say they made your eyes go funny after a bit! In this piece I am using many stories I have heard over the years about working in a chocolate factory – stories both from my dad and from other workers.

The Chocolate Angel (p.160) – I do believe there are angels for every occasion! I hope mine is the chocolate one, I think I deserve that at least! Chocolate seems to inspire such happy memories for me, like mam making toffee apples. My mother's take on chocolate would always be very different to my dad's, as I hope this piece shows. My mum never worked in a factory – but she was an extremely good cook. She cooked in the war and also in service in London.

Dad and Terry's Factory (p.161) – This is simply a true story about what happened to my dad in those mercilessly strict times of work in the twenties. He had some very unlucky things happen work-wise.

Uncle Pa's Drawer (p.162) – This is about the drawer my Uncle kept in our front room. All the things I describe really were there. He would give me Caramac as a special treat. He was a very clever quick-witted man and also the fastest walker in York.

The Empress of Chocolate (p.162) – This is an imagined lady based on the Emperor of Ice Cream. I imagine she lives at Pompeii. An Italian feel to this poem, I hope. There are so many personalities to chocolate – difficult to capture them all.

Les Petits Chiens de Paris (p.163) – This is dedicated to all the wonderful dogs you see in Paris. I have often drawn them, but they are so exquisite I thought they should have a poem as well. Of the many chocolate shops you see there – you see as many little French dogs being trotted in and out of them.

The Chocolate Bird in the Garden (p.164) – I like to give chocolate a real persona. Why not a bird, birds are so free, I often write them into poems. My favourite image I think.

— from *Here's Looking at You, Kid* (2014) —

Here's Looking at You, Kid (p.165) – This is essentially a poem about where I grew up in York. It could be difficult sometimes, if you went to a different school in the area – much of what you do that is different doesn't always make for an easy life. The phrase 'here's looking at you, kid' is of course from Casablanca – a film my dad and I often watched together, and a phrase we often used between us, so it brings back very happy memories. People have said they like the fact that the sun is being kept safe in the father's pocket.

Dad's Lingo (p.166) – This poem was part of a series of poems looking at different 'lingos' we use in our everyday lives. Because all his family came from County Mayo, dad was incredibly proud of his Irish heritage. This is simply the extraordinary language that my father spoke in. He was a complete contradiction in terms, unfathomable and his language, like his handwriting, was rich, ornate and often wildly funny. Sometimes my mother would say that dad and I both spoke in Irish – meaning that, if asked whether we knew the way to somewhere, our answer might well be: 'Yes, but I wouldn't start from here!' There is a different turn of mind with all things Celtic I feel – and I have tried to capture a suggestion of it here. A lot of Irish listeners have been kind enough to really like and endorse the poem.

The Kids with the Tree House (p.167) – This poem was a true story, in part, about a very 'posh' area near where I lived as a kid – and an infamous visit to the glorious tree house mentioned. I always wanted a tree house, my whole childhood. The house with the fancy driveway is still there, we pass it occasionally.

Hospital Lingo (p.167) – This is another 'lingo' poem. I have had a lot of dealings on the health front over the years, and rarely write about this area of life – but thought here I would make an exception. I tried to make something light-hearted, but also something that people could connect and relate to, and it does seem to do that. People can identify with elements and seem to have a really good laugh – so, I hope you can also.

French Cat in French Window (p.169) – This has become a bit of a party piece, and is a poem often asked for by people. I like to read in different accents – and this one is done in a mock French, Clouseau-esque accent, which is I have to admit is great fun to do. This poem was written about a real cat my partner Phil and I saw in a French restaurant window in the Latin Quarter. I love Paris especially – and find the Parisians have great style and a great attitude, as well as being very kind. This cat seemed to develop his own voice as I wrote the poem – and I like to think of him as still there, running his restaurant in the Bois de Boulogne. Maybe, one day, he'll let me have a table...

The Serving Girl (p.170) – This poem is dedicated to my grandmother, Margaret Mack, who was brought up in Bootle, Liverpool. She travelled round Britain with her brothers who worked as navvies, and she also worked as a serving girl in local houses. (My mother later followed in this manner and went into service in London, in Chelsea – so in a way this poem is about both of them.) It won a Commended Prize in the 2014 Ware Poetry Competition. She was a very strong woman by all accounts and I wish I had known her. My mother looked after her when she was very ill and always said she heard angels singing as she climbed the stairs to her room to find she had died. This poem is taken from a photograph I have of her which I think is quite beautiful.

The Old Pig (p.172) – This poem won the Torbay Open Poetry Prize in 2013. It is a true story my mother told of an old pig that she looked after on the family farm in Doncaster. She told the story many times to me, and she would have been so proud to hear this poem won a prize. When I read it, I can hear her voice telling me the story – and briefly she is back with me. She was a real country girl at heart.

The Kindness Medal (p.173) – This poem goes in tandem with the 'Wild Mother' poem, as I think my mum was always innately kind to people. As is the way with kindness, it doesn't seem to get much of a reward in life. The medal I show when reading this poem is a medal mum got in Rome to commemorate the opening of the Holy Door in 1950. I have had many comments from people about this poem – it seems to really strike an emotional chord for them. Perhaps we are all aware of the kindness we meet in life – and want to sing its praises?

My Wild Mother (p.174) – This was a poem written after my mum had died, although I think she saw an early draft of it. I like to think bits of it would have made her laugh – although she would probably have been scandalised by other parts of it! I was very pleased for it to be included in the *Iron Anthology of Humorous Verse*, up in Newcastle. I have had a lot of requests for copies of this poem as people often come up and say – 'Yes! That's my mother!' So it seems there are a lot of wild and rebellious mothers out there. Just as well ...

The Christmas Letter (p.176) – This has always been a very popular poem, it won the Waterstones poetry prize Judged by Gervase Phinn. It began life in response to a letter we receive every Christmas, a round-robin letter, and also because so many people were now sending huge Christmas missives with their cards.

Eight o'clock in Britain (p.178) – This poem was published on a Hollywood blogzine site (the nearest I've got to Hollywood so far!) and is really a tongue-in-cheek piece about how Britain seems to shut down somewhat earlier than cities in Europe. I like the longer days and evenings that Europe has, and wish more of that would happen here. That feeling of having more time, and the possibility to do what you want in it – that would be good!

All you need is love (p.180) – I find a lot of the Beatles' lyrics very inspirational, and this poem came out of that enjoyment. Poets always write about love in one way or another, so it was tricky to try and find a new angle. I think listening to sixties music helped – and this poem has its own particular rhythm. People seem to enjoy its diversity and approach, and I hope one day to read it at the Casbah Club, where the Beatles first played, in Liverpool. I visited there for my birthday and touched the lucky dragon on the wall. I always say I have never really left the sixties.

Sixties Anthem (p.182) – It incorporates a lot of ridiculous things I did in the Sixties. That feeling of 'anything goes' – and of being in the moment, just being alive – is what I wanted to capture here. I have taken a bit of poetic license with some of the facts! This was based on a real event when I went recklessly hitch hiking. My Aunt Chrissy lived in Leeds and I remember she gave us some ice cream soda before we left and a piece of fruit cake.

Baxter's Crime (p.183) – This poem was published in a micro-chapbook in America by Origami Poems. It was written about a real dog that seemed to be walked regularly down the back street behind my house. I heard him everyday, though never saw him, so he became a distant friend. People often seem to identify with Baxter, as described in the poem – and I know I do. He has now had several illustrations done of him as well. I think he will feature in a story eventually.

The Kindness of Dogs (p.184) – I often seem to write poems about dogs. Like birds, they represent freedom and playfulness to me. A phrase of my dad's was 'I'm not bad for a two-year-old dog…' and I concur with this. The kind nature of dogs is what I hoped to capture here – and if you have a dog yourself, I hope you like it.

Distance (p.185) – This poem was written shortly after my dad had died. I still miss his extraordinary sense of humour and storytelling ability, which was remarkable. I remember he told me he would 'hang on' for as long as he could, but when he was gone, he would still be thinking of me. He said there is a light that shines for me, in the darkness – and that I was not to be sad. I hope he would have liked this poem, and what I try to achieve through all of the poems. The stories we write with our hearts are what matter. It is about trying to come to terms with the death of someone, my dad in this case. I don't know if I believe in all this 'just sleeping' lark. Wherever he is I'm sure it will be down the pub.

A wheelchair goes into a bar (p.185) – This is the true story of the last twelve years or so of having to use a wheelchair. Sometimes we can laugh ... and sometimes not. A lot of the anecdotes are based on fact, and although I don't write about this subject very much, here I thought I had found a way for the subject to still be entertaining as well as making people think.

The Open Door (p.187) – This poem was written one day when I really wanted to get out of the house, and due to health issues, I couldn't. Birds often feature in my work, as I love the freedom they represent. Keeping doors open, both literally and in the mind is what keeps a writer alive I think. When people get this poem they really 'get' it – and I would like to think it's a stepping stone for someone moving through a not so great moment, heading towards a more hopeful one.

The Lucky Dip Machine of the Magic Bird of Fortune (p.188) – This poem has become a firm favourite for people to read at times of romantic celebration. I believe it has been greatly enjoyed at weddings. It was inspired by my amazing partner Phil. He is the best thing that ever happened to me. If only we had met sooner, like when we were four ... we hope that will be the case next time. There really is such a thing as a soul mate.

My Mother, the Mustang (p.189) – I love images of wild horses and often draw them. With their tremendous independence, mystery and wildness, they seem to represent the very essence of my mother, who was a woman of great strength and character – but who also was always impossible to fully describe. A delightful enigma! This poem is about my mum's last couple of days in hospital. She seemed to still be speaking to me to the very end. Her language was so wild compared to my own.

What They Found in the Poet's Stomach (p.190) – This poem, and the next, were written in 2014 especially for the Keats Shelley House in Rome. I have based this first one not only on the very short but brilliant life of Keats, but also what it is about poetry that draws us to write. No one chooses to be a poet I think, and quite often we stand upon the shoulders of poets who have gone before us. Keats, I believe, was a poet who almost carried too high an ideal about the art of poetry. He was in a sense a guardian of the state of poetry – and this is a hard task to be set for any young poet. Keats said "I cannot live without poetry."

Keats in Piazza Navona (p.191) – Piazza Navona is one of my favourite squares in Rome, as it is a great people-watching arena. I imagine Keats coming back to life there, and enjoying all that Roman life has to offer – the vibrancy, the colour, the beauty. Phil and I had the world's worst lasagne here, and way too pricey. Keats would have fared better I am sure. Although rumour has it he hated pasta. This poem was written especially to perform at Keats Shelley house in Rome.

Watcher of the Skies (p.192) – I was privileged to be asked to judge the Keats-Shelley Prize for Young People, and this poem was written to perform for the bicentenary of Keats. I did a fair bit of research about him when I went to Keats House in Rome thanks to the kindness and courtesy of Giuseppe Albano. When Keats was a youngster and in his school playground, he was very fond of watching the skies, turning round and round to do so. He had a keen interest in the sky and I hope he would have liked this poem.

The Romany Ghosts of My Father (p.193) – This poem is a particular favourite of mine as it relates specifically to my dad's family, who all came across from County Mayo. They were a big Catholic family and mainly settled in the Walmgate district of York – which was really a little Ireland. Some eventually emigrated to New York and Boston, while others settled more locally in Leeds. The poem came to me all of a piece, and was like a refrain in my head for some days. It has often been performed to music, and I would like to perform it one day in Mayo.

The Green Piano (p.195) – This is the poem I am asked for most. People always want a copy of it – I have read it at literary events, folk festivals and cabarets, and it seems to appeal to all ages and all backgrounds. It's about living every moment of your life just as it comes and *to the full*. It was written all of a single piece, sat in my conservatory one sunny afternoon.

Starting Over (p.196) – This poem is for my partner, Phil, without whom very few of these poems would have been written – he is my "Bridge Over Troubled Water". He is what makes the day complete and allows me to continue to tinker at the green piano of poetry that is always playing in my mind. Here's looking at you, kid – here's looking at you.

— from *Americana* (2015) —

The letter that never came for the old song and dance man (p.197) – This poem was written, as so many poems are about my dad Billy Burke. The story was always told to me that his family were waiting for a letter from Johnny Burke from America – to send for them all to go and live in the U.S. And that this letter somehow went astray – one of the great regrets of my dad's life was not seeing America. He loved all things American and would, I know, have flourished there.

Route 66 (p.198) – This poem is about being taken out into Chicago to see the Route 66 sign by friends Melanie, Mike and Bob. We were absolutely shattered with jet lag and couldn't really take in the fact we had arrived.

The Cakes at Walts (p.198) – This poem was written about the cakes on display in the local Chicago supermarket – it was the 4th July – and I have never seen cakes this size. People were snapping them up like crazy – we couldn't believe what we were seeing!

The Basement Kids (p.200) – This poem was dedicated to the whole basement culture, which is alive and well and full of American kids. Never having had a basement – this whole realm was new to us – and it has to be said … a little bit scary.

Fireflies in Melanie's Garden (p.201) – This was the evening of 4th July celebrations – and fireflies were out in force. I had never seen one before and was captivated by their sudden ballet in the garden.

Racoon Runs for President (p.202) – And America was also full of new wildlife – previously undreamt of wildlife for us. On our friends' porch racoons come out and play and for a time one was living under the porch. Sitting out there was a bit like taking a 'Walk on the Wild Side'!

Bob Goes for Popcorn (p.203) – And also in Chicago we went with friend Bob to a little bar for chilli dogs and chips. There was a popcorn machine on the wall – which was a new idea to us – everything in a new country is strange and amazing.

The Chicago Drug Guy (p.204) – We were waiting to see a concert in the main park in Chicago when a man approached us supposedly to ask the time. We discovered later – this is a pseudonym for drug dealers to suss people out.

That Lady Liberty (p.204) – This was a poem simply written about the concept of freedom and liberty – something my father and I always admired about America. It was – as we believed – a place where people could be equal and have a chance to make something of their lives.

The Cuban Lady (p.205) – This was a lady who had been a dancer, we met her when we flew in to La Guardia New York airport. She was a most unusual character – and then suddenly an ambulance arrived to take her away. As a first experience of a New York story – this made quite an impression on us.

So, what's the deal New York? (p.205) – This was a poem written about New York while we were in New York doing a performance of poetry at The New Yorker Hotel in the centre. Impossible to capture New York in any one image – I had to settle for a butterfly in the end. The city still amazes and baffles me – it has so many aspects to it.

Empire State Violation (p.206) – We went to the top of the Empire State Building – and were frisked and searched several times en route – the whole experience was, given that we were told to move away from the elevator – all in all, a little bit scary. I use the key word violation as we heard this word so often whilst in America.

In Which I Dream of Rats (p.207) – Yet another poem about New York – the whole city seems to be a living breathing musical or poem in many ways. Everyone is scurrying somewhere – so I guess I had the image of rats, fast moving and furious along the sidewalks. There seemed to be a tidal wave of people coming at us all the time – I had no idea it would be so incredibly manic. You almost feel you can't breathe. A native New Yorker told me on Rhode Island – the place is just too intense.

Pushing (p.208) – Everyone in the city seems to be either wheeling a trolley or a rack of something from point A to point B – we weren't sure what these items were most of the time. Like pantomime horses – galloping madly – unreal and you forget they are humans!

The John Lennon Doorman (p.209) – We eventually found the Imagine memorial – and also the hotel over the way where John Lennon was shot. To say the doorman was fiercely disinterested would be an understatement.

A Few Dollars More (p.210) – And so we got the Amtrak train from New York on to Rhode Island – where we met with friends, Jan and Kevin Keough. This poem was inspired by a phrase about money I heard a lady say in Providence, Rhode Island.

Heatwave, Rhode Island (p.210) – An incredible heatwave hit Rhode Island while we were there. Almost impossible to walk around.

Joleen, Joleen (p.211) – This was the lady who cleaned our room at the hotel on Rhode Island. She also served us breakfast – and appeared to do just about everything else around the place.

The Man on Wickenden Street (p.212) – We went into a record shop and asked about some sixties and seventies vinyl LPs – but the guy serving obviously thought we weren't cool enough to bother with!

Emily's Dress (p.212) – It had been a long held dream of mine to visit Emily Dickinson's house at Amherst. Thanks to friends Jan Keough and Mary Mueller – we were able to go! We had hired a car which decided not to work the whole time of our visit. The house itself was very atmospheric and I always feel a very close fellow feeling with Emily Dickinson. Her lines seem to be dusted with a little bit of magic dust – they are so unexpected and often inexplicably wonderful.

In Emily Dickinson's Garden (p.214) – I just wanted to write a piece here that celebrated Emily and her wonderful garden which she attended to such a lot herself – this seemed the right way to do it. The sight of the majestic white oak planted her brother that survived a great storm was an image that will always stay with me. The spirit of Emily seems to also survive in the garden and house.

Americano Pizza (p.215) – I am not generally a fan of the quick pizza – and this was us bewailing not being able to find an Indian restaurant near where we stayed on Rhode Island. This was written all of a piece as we walked along the bay behind the hotel – one of our last nights spent in America.

Better Late Than Never (p.216) – And – as always – it's best to let my dad have the last word on America. I am sure he accompanied us on the whole of the journey – why wouldn't he? This was his dream journey being fulfilled at last. I hope he would have been proud of myself and Phil – and might feel that he had at long last seen America. You really shouldn't let a little thing like death stop you! In the words of his hero Jimmy Cagney: "My mother thanks you. My father thanks you. And I thank you."

— from the Origami Poems Project (2010-2016) —

The Whisper of Birds (p.217) – Written in the garden at Melbourne Street about the many visiting blackbirds, watching them build a nest and being envious.

The Russian Doll that Was My Mother (p.218) – Written about the enigmatic nature of my mother. I thought the image of Russian dolls perfectly symbolised the many layers of which she was made. She was an enigma wrapped in a mystery!

Walking the Dog (p.218) – I wrote this in Totleigh Barton, down in Devon, one of the Arvon centres. I was down there on a course with the wonderful Michael Donaghy; I wrote this and 'The City' during that course. He would always say when you met with him, with a glinting Irish look in his eye: 'What are you writing? How's the work?'

Beer (p.219) – This poem was inspired by my taxi driver friend Mal Caddie. He wrote a poem called 'Beer' as well, and the two poems were put to a vote to see which was the best – with the other taxi drivers doing the voting. His won by miles, and to this day he maintains he is the far superior poet.

The Midnight Boat (p.219) – This was written about the afternoon my mum died. She loved boats, and on the wall of the hospital was a painting of a felucca, an Egyptian sailboat, on which the ancient Egyptians would sail off into the afterlife. Just as I was looking at that, they called me to say she had taken a turn for the worst. (My mother once met Egyptologist Howard Carter, when she was working in London.)

The Moon Crying (p.220) – This was written on the isle of Leros, my second trip. I had gone on a three-week holiday looking for the wild orchid of Leros; I was the only one who found it, much to the annoyance of the other snooty orchid-hunters.

Bonsai (p.220) – The Bonsai in this poem is myself, during a difficult time in life.

The Blind Dog (p.221) – The dog in question belonged to one of Phil's customers, and I was moved to write it by the stories of what the dog did during the day.

The Littlest Hobo (p.222) – I've always loved the TV series of the same name, and quite fancied travelling from town to town, a la Woody Guthrie, jumping trains – which I did on one memorable occasion, to avoid paying a ticket, having got in trouble for impersonating a werewolf in first class.

The Leaves of Dachau (p.223) – This poem is about surviving against all odds, and with dignity.

The Last Time (p.224) – The last time I saw my father was 4.20pm on the 13th March 1999. Extraordinary though it sounds, every year he finds a way to communicate with me at that time. During my last meeting with Jamie about this book, there was one last poem I hadn't written a note for – this one – and sure enough, as Jamie brought the poem up on his laptop, it was 4.20pm on the 13th March.

Two Dreams (p.224) – This is really just about how the difference in dreams very much depends on our state of mind and interpretation. Mine nowadays are often juxtaposed in this way. I have always dreamt in colour.

Visiting the Parrot (p.225) – I visited a friend who was looking after a parrot briefly. My conversation with the bird was the deeper one! I relate strongly to birds, horses and donkeys and dogs. I am more animal bird than poet I feel. See my wings?

What I Meant to Do (p.226) – This is simply 'a seize the day' revelation. Get the hell on with it … you don't know how long you've got, so run up that mountain and smile at yourself, your lunacy and do it all at least twenty-two times a day!

All I Want (p.226) – This is me and Phil and nothing else matters really, in this whole hill of beans, to quote Rick in *Casablanca*. Phil is my free world, my love, my all and more.

Moments (p.227) – This is the analysis of the everyday, as it runs through our lives. Wondrous and rich and challenging. You should never try to analyse the moment too deeply, simply become the moment. Like a good Abba song let it fill your whole body up with joy and immediacy.

The Healing Pool (p.228) – This has been recorded by friend Kevin Keough. I am really pleased and so delighted he wanted to look at this poem in musical terms. I love music, but the creation of new music puts me in awe at how this may be done. Kevin and Jan and I have spoken often of healing for myself and for others. They have been an incredible support to Phil and I in very difficult times and are our friends of the soul.

Different Snowdrops (p.228) – This is about looking at whatever wood you may be travelling through and trying to understand how life has led you there. Beauty lives in each and every wood, every snowdrop, every bluebell. Says me who was always a city gal!

Indigo (p.229) – This is about having the healing power of indigo brought to me. In whatever way that may be.

Inside a Dog's Head (p.230) – This poem is simply about the qualities of dogs as I see it. The pure unrivalled beauty of a simple life, well lived, well barked. A dreaming dog lying peacefully in the sunshine, legs still running. Dedicated to Wendy, Pixie, and Molly dog. And Emma, Mary Ann's dog.

Dances With Dogs (p.231) – This is a fun piece dedicated to one of my cousins on my mum's side of the family, who really did used to come in and dance with Flossie the dog.

The Sulking Dog (p.232) – I was talking about dogs with friend Mary Mueller and as ever the humour of the dog comedian inspired this poem.

Man Sweeping Leaves (p.232) – This poem has proved to be a very popular poem with diverse groups of people. Written about Phil sweeping our back yard, of course. You can learn a lot about a man by the way he sweeps. That sounds a bit Neil Young-ish – or am I dreaming?

Once I Knew (p.233) – What you believe about yourself may not be the whole sum of things. But the whole of what you believe even less so. Am I an apple, a dancer, a rainbow … or all these things rolled into one? The trouble is I want to know now, and then to forget it utterly, otherwise how do we move on from here to that green field I long for.

Snowed In (p.234) – This was written in Wales, about a cottage I used to stay at called Cilrhye in Mid Wales. The poem was written about a day I was looking through the window and talking to a dear friend Alex. I hope she would have liked the poem. She died far too young but packed a lot into those years. I often think of her and dedicate this piece to her.

The Poolside Babes (p.234) – This poem was very much enjoyed, I'm told, by friends in America at various gatherings and barbecues and parties. It's a fun piece and based on observations by a pool in Corfu. As informative as sitting in a bar!

The Dogs of Corfu (p.235) – This is about some dogs that scared Phil and I as we headed for a bus into Corfu town. I wouldn't want to meet them at night.

Under the Old Tree, Corfu Town (p.236) – This is a very special poem, it is where Phil and I have arranged to meet up, after I am gone. "All shall be well, and all shall be well and all manner of thing shall be well." (Julian of Norwich)

A Certain Kind of Mist (p.237) – About the vagaries of life as they assail us. And inspired by Emily Dickinson once more as I seem to see her through the mist darkly triumphant once again. My favourite line of hers is "Not all Pianos in the Woods / Had power to mangle me."

Picasso Woman (p.238) – About my favourite artist. He changed my visual view of the world in a way I cannot comprehend or fully understand. Matisse, Dali, Vermeer all draw me in too, but Picasso seems to echo something in me. Why, I cannot fathom. He resists all analysis and I love that he does.

Glass Robins (p.238) – Phil has a special affiliation with robins that we always joke about. Robins disappear if I appear and blackbirds appear for me. The robin is the spirit messenger; maybe he has too many messages for me.

Ballad of Penny Lane (p.239) – This was written after a day in Liverpool. I think of my granny living in Bootle and Birkenhead, and I wish I had lived there in the sixties. Doesn't everyone?! Those songs are part of our DNA.

Ringo's House (p.240) – Written after day in Liverpool going round Mendips and Paul's house and lastly Ringo's on the way home. An unforgettable day.

The Trees at the Cemetery (p.242) – About taking flowers up to my parent's grave in York Cemetery. A cemetery is always an evocative place.

Flowers by the Roadside (p.243) – About this new strange habit of people of placing small graves wherever people die. We are not especially keen on this and the poem hopefully registers this. No wish to offend, but I think its best the air commemorates in all its wild wisdom and beauty.

Climbing Trees (p.244) – About Phil climbing trees more than me, I think. He has shown me the real beauty of tree climbing and one day we will climb, as Lennon says, to the top, to the tippety top and never stop.

If I had never seen a butterfly (p.246) – This is a very recent poem inspired by butterflies and Emily Dickinson somehow. I have a strong connection to Emily Dickinson and visited her house when in America. She would also have to have been invented if she had not existed. She has given the world of poetry wings.

The Valley of Happy Songs (p.246) – I was pleased to send this to Mike Jenkins, a wonderful Welsh poet friend down in Merthyr Tydfil. Wales has held some very happy memories for me over the years, my other granny, not the Irish one, was Welsh, actually could be my Great Gran, I reckon. My mam always said she was a real tartar. Dressed in black and very correct. Sometimes I have a Welsh voice that switches on when I write, I can always tell because it's like music and a conversation.

New Childhood (p.247) – This is about some difficult times and my gratitude to Phil for seeing me through them. I was told in October 2015, when we first started work on this book, that I would die in hospital; then was sent home to die. At the moment, however, I am still here, and we take every day as it comes along. Just happy to still be together.

Leaving Messages in Trees (p.248) – This is a true saga about the whimsical little kid I was, who left messages in the trees in Heslington Low Moor. Heck, they were the only trees I was likely to see. I still feel that trees speak their message out into the world with vision and peace and love. Once an old hippy … I wish I could have lived in a tree house overlooking the ocean with a dog called Zorro at my feet.

Index of first lines

A butterfly, a white butterfly lands on my arm   214
Against the hut that the boatman keeps   80
All I want, before the end   226
All life, all love, all laughter is here   191
All the kids in New York, are looking after rats.   207
Always on a Friday it happened –   158
And... some people spend their whole lives, snowed in.   234
And best of all –   41
And it's always just like that.   104
And it reached out that long arm   188
And there was.   153
An echo has reached me   79
are edgy fledglings.   95
are everywhere.   163
Are keen. Lean. Lean and mean, sometimes.   234
As a child, a fanciful child – (still am)   248
As if they are.   238
As if to mask death a bunch of dahlias   243
A small dog is slipping in and out   39
At crucial moments of my life   134
At first, at the Foreigners' Club   145
At the top of the long hill, when the dust settles,   40
Autumn is falling outside,   19
A wheelchair goes into a bar and   185
Baxter, the dog, is being dragged down the lane.   183
Be careful of May.   24
'Be careful of the tiles,' he said.   118
Beer is you. Beer is you Against All Odds.   219
Billy at the cemetery oversees the dead.   85
Bob goes for popcorn – and he says,   203
Cilla dances, and there   29
Come May – when roses bloom   41
Cutting the road   64
Dad was three minutes late at the factory gate.   161

Dear both, 102
Dear Father and God and all them Saints – 101
Dear Peach, 120
Different snowdrops, different lives; 228
Digging ourselves further into the sand, 36
Does everything with a flounce. 232
Do not count the days, but rather *live* them. 195
Down to the waterfall and back 56
Emily's dress stands at the top of the stairs 212
Even in chocolate, there is a hierarchy. 159
Everyone in New York is pushing something. 208
First, take an unusual childhood. 81
Foxgloves are a wild flower. 73
George sits on the corner of 61
Give a man a map 52
Hallo. 176
Has arisen this morning over the field… and 237
He asks us if we got the time, 204
He is American. 99
He is an uncommon priest – our first sighting. 46
He is a Peter Pan of the disco scene. 72
He is savvy. Smart as a whip, and savvy. 209
He knew his place in the toy room. 156
Here in the dangerously warm burden of the night 210
Here we sit, and are happy. 236
He was old, you told me. 172
How it reminds me of you, that horse language. 189
How we hated them. 167
I'm on coats 66
I am catching the last of the sun 30
I am the Empress of Chocolate – and 162
I am the Littlest Hobo. 222
I believe in chocolate. 154
I cannot understand why you are so heavy. 121
I did not know there were two layers to you, island. 47
I do not want to answer the door. 221

I dreamed I was a horse   143
If I remember correctly   182
I had intended to look at the roses today, but   226
I have taken to drawing dogs.   149
I have walked round them all today,   20
I know there is a beginning and an end to most things   50
Imagine.   34
Inch by inch, they emerge.   132
In other languages   19
I noticed from an early age that the sun   165
In their defence I will say this.   242
In their hurry,   48
In the kitchen   114
In the space that surrounds apples – there is a hint of banana   113
In this our new religion   247
I remember the first time   239
I sleep fully-clothed in case   60
It's always eight o'clock in Britain.   178
It's always the last one on the tour   240
'It's as though something is   55
'It's not so bad,' he calls out.   57
It's something to do with the way   140
It came in a cheap box,   220
It is a pageant of owls.   76
It seems a strange sort of night to any other.   220
It was always that letter.   197
It was great.   106
I wonder   126
Joleen is our room cleaner, we meet her in the lift   211
Kathleen runs down to see the ferry;   45
Laugh and see   34
Life is just a series of moments.   227
Like mountains they are simply there –   120
Like some old Injun – that was me dad.   157
Like the Russian Doll we kept on the sideboard –   218
Listen out for me,   42

Love is not the old lady at home all alone,   17
Mam believed in angels.   160
Maybe, one day,   229
Maybe I had no business there,   88
Mother,   150
must have been wrong;   18
My city is floating. It seemed like fun at first.   117
My cousin it was, became known as   231
My dad is packing his suitcase for America   216
My father's optimism on driving   91
My last night in Leros,   49
My mother's at that difficult age   174
My mother's lighter head has arrived   110
My steps have no shadows.   130
Never go first when landing on the moon.   98
New York – is a poet.   205
Next to the bird-table,   32
No one wants to be the first to go.   63
No one wears beige on the fourteenth deck.   146
Nothing ever happens.   83
Once he was all dog –   100
Outside, the snow is singing –   125
People walking by the water's edge are   22
Please stop putting tortoises through my letterbox.   119
Sandra is five foot two.   138
She calls it 'the dining room'. I hear 'the dying room'.   116
She drowned kittens. Laid people out.   21
Sheep are odd.   58
She is blonde, about sixty, very pretty.   205
She likes her men second-hand.   86
She picks you out – that Lady Liberty,   204
So, it's like this.   232
So. I am a French cat in a French window and you   169
Soft as tissue paper the tree smiles.   244
So many stars tonight   48
Someone's breath has been left here   31

So much goes unheeded. 97
Standing outside the glass phone booth 23
Star-gazer Towers, Barnsley East, Monday. 70
Stories are what make us who we are. 187
Tells me that today, it is spring. 164
That room. 128
The basement kids, with their basement smiles 200
The boat that bears your name, she is midnight. 219
The bones of the old house 108
The cakes at Walts are huge – no, bigger than that. 198
The day is all moon and roses 46
The day is a rose, a white rose again and here 38
The day you notice 18
The last time I saw my father I think we spoke about blackbirds. 224
The Master says 92
The people of my father's days 69
There's a lot of it about 167
There are three words 230
There is no 'of course' about love. 180
The route through the churchyard 33
The sea is a single blue banana 35
These days (forgive me) 122
These folk are refugees from the Land of Chocolate. 155
The snake has surrounded itself, it is beside itself 74
The valley of happy songs is where I want to live. 246
The world would be broken and smaller 246
They are prepared to dig a little deeper, 59
The yellow man and the priest 43
They live near me, the chocolate girls 103
They say – 193
They sit about my house, the aunts – 28
They were narrow, beautiful. 25
They write words in the night air and we 201
This dog, India, has many faces, many masters. 75
This heat is Rothko hot, 210
This is a medal for kind people. 173

This is his home town only because   87
This is no speedy seeing off,   78
This is recuperation then, this is rehabilitation.   147
This is the language of leaves.   223
This says it all – the whisper from the trees.   217
Though I never knew her   170
Through the window I could see the small cage,   225
Timothy the tapir –   93
Tired and jet-lagged, our first day in America   198
Today,   133
Today, again, I am her.   238
Today I am avoiding stories, but everywhere I go things happen.   136
To explain it better – Mike brings two skulls out.   202
Tomorrow, there will be enough   151
Tonight,   144
Tonight, I am the sea,   77
Tonight, we eat pizza like wolves.   215
Trees, hundreds of them,   127
Two dreams I had, and not sure which to believe.   224
Uncle's drawer was full of it – chocolate of every size   162
Under an almost moon-landscape at Aldeburgh,   65
Watch out for them.   123
We are in a violation, and this is a shooting offence.   206
We are lying just below where the swallows lie,   37
We discussed   68
We go into the shop. His record shop.   212
We hear them barking in the night. All night.   235
We queued to be a part of it.   26
We stood beneath the candles,   44
We were almost engaged,   51
We will start over again.   196
What is it? How should I call it?   185
What they found in the poet's stomach   190
When I am gone   122
When I was a dancer, then   233
When the pain comes and my warrior legs   124

When they tell you I am gone –   192
When will I take you, I ask –   152
Where the wild Oxalis blooms,   44
Why should I speak of pain?   218
Yesterday was not a good day.   228
You always hurried me on past them.   112
You ask me what his lingo was   166
You can't miss it.   96
You can't see the sunset   90
You come in to the shop with me and   141
You had a special way   54
You say it and it is true.   184
'You will, won't you – you WILL stay in touch,' she said.   148
You wrote to me of storms,   62

Index of titles

A Certain Kind of Mist   237
A Few Dollars More   210
Aghia Marina   38
Aldeburgh   65
Alinda Bay   39
All I Want   226
All you need is love   180
Americano Pizza   215
And God Said Let There Be Chocolate   153
Ankle-Deep   36
Another Song   64
Arrival – Leros   34
At Elvington   33
At Garbo's   45
At Highfield   32
At the Castle   40
At the Foreigners' Club   145
Avoiding Stories   136
A wheelchair goes into a bar   185
Ballad of Penny Lane   239
Batsi, Andros   22
Baxter's Crime   183
Be Careful   118
Beer   219
Better Late Than Never   216
Billy   85
Bless This Handbag   134
Boatman   80
Bob Goes for Popcorn   203
Bonsai   220
Children's Games   104
Children's Hospice   116

Chocolate Credo   154
Climbing Trees   244
Dad's Lingo   166
Dad and Terry's Factory   161
Dances With Dogs   231
Dawn   41
Dear Rucksack   121
Departure   48
Different Snowdrops   228
Distance   185
Donor   122
Drawing Dogs   149
Eight o'clock in Britain   178
Emily's Dress   212
Empire State Violation   206
Enlightenment   92
Fever Flowers   59
Fireflies in Melanie's Garden   201
Fireworks   54
Flowers by the Roadside   243
For Bob (in Leros)   44
Foreigner   23
Foxglove   73
French Cat in French Window   169
Full Fruit Salad   120
Gargunnock   79
George   61
Glass Robins   238
Good Advice   97
Head   110
Heart   20
Heatwave, Rhode Island   210
Here – Now   34

Here's Looking at You, Kid   165
Home Town   87
Hope Street   69
Hospital Lingo   167
How to Spot a Poet   123
If I had never seen a butterfly   246
India   75
Indigo   229
In Emily Dickinson's Garden   214
In May   24
In My Day   122
Inside a Dog's Head   230
In Which Dad is 'Dances With Chocolate'   157
In Which I Dream of Rats   207
Irish Funeral   78
Joleen, Joleen   211
Kallinichta   49
Keats in Piazza Navona   191
Lacing Boots   25
Lazarus Enrolls at the Gym   88
Leaving   63
Leaving Messages in Trees   248
Leros Cat-Walk   47
Les Petits Chiens de Paris   163
Love is the Feeling Between Now and Now   17
Making Ends Meet   99
Man Sweeping Leaves   232
Map   52
Mellow Yellow   72
Message   102
Moments   227
My Mother, the Mustang   189
My Red Sandals   130

My Wild Mother   174
Neil, Honey   98
New Childhood   247
New Girl at the Shop   51
Once I Knew   233
On Coats   66
On the 14th Deck of the Cruise Ship Aurora   146
On Wearing My Uncle Patrick's Hat   126
Owls   144
Oz   62
Papa Retsina   46
Patmos   46
Piano   19
Picasso Woman   238
Poem for Mrs Waters   21
Pushing   208
Quiet Auditorium   125
Racing Caterpillars   132
Racoon Runs for President   202
Recipe for a Poet   81
Ringo's House   240
Route 66   198
Saint George's Chapel   44
Sandra is a Child of Peace and Love   138
Sea-Largo   77
Second-hand Men   86
Sheep   58
Silver Wedding   96
Sixties Anthem   182
Snake   74
Snowed In   234
So, what's the deal New York?   205

Space 55
Starting Over 196
Stay in Touch 148
Strange Meeting 112
Sun 30
Sundays 101
Swallows at Aghia 37
That Lady Liberty 204
The Apple House 108
The Aunts 28
The Back of Beyond 90
The Basement Kids 200
The Blind Dog 221
The Blue Cooker 114
The Cakes at Walts 198
The Chicago Drug Guy 204
The Chocolate Angel 160
The Chocolate Bird in the Garden 164
The Chocolate Girls 103
The Christmas Letter 176
The City 76
The Creature from the Chocolate Lagoon 158
The Cuban Lady 205
The Dancing Room 128
The Dog in the Painting 100
The Dogs of Corfu 235
The Empress of Chocolate 162
The Film 26
The Flying Suit 60
The Gift 133
The Green Field 143
The Green Piano 195
The Grenz 127
The Happening 83

The Healing Pool 228
The John Lennon Doorman 209
The Kids with the Tree House 167
The Kindness Medal 173
The Kindness of Dogs 184
The Last Time 224
The Leaves of Dachau 223
The Lens of the Camera 18
The letter that never came for the old song and dance man 197
The Little Chocolate Soldier 156
The Littlest Hobo 222
The Lucky Dip Machine of the Magic Bird of Fortune 188
The Man on Wickenden Street 212
The Midnight Boat 219
The Moon Crying 220
The Old Pig 172
The Op 57
The Open Door 187
The Other House 124
The Point of Men 120
The Poolside Babes 234
The Prepared Room 31
Therapy 70
The Refuseniks 155
The Rehabilitation Hobbies Room 147
The Road Out of Town 152
The Romany Ghosts of My Father 193
The Ruby Slippers 141
The Russian Doll that Was My Mother 218

The Serving Girl   170
The Shape of Hands   150
The Skyline   18
The Smarties Room   159
The Space Around   113
The Sulking Dog   232
The Test   91
The Traveller   42
The Trees at the Cemetery   242
The Valley of Happy Songs   246
The Whisper of Birds   217
The York Floods   117
Tigers   50
Timothy   93
Tomorrow   151
Tortoises   119
Town People on a Beach   95
Two Dreams   224
Uncle Pa's Drawer   162
Under the Old Tree, Corfu Town   236
V.E. Day   41
Villa   43
Visiting the Parrot   225
Vortex   48
Walkers   56
Walking the Dog   218
Watcher of the Skies   192
Welcome   19
Whale   68
What I Meant to Do   226
What They Found in the Poet's
   Stomach   190
When Dad was Father Christmas   106
Why I Fancy Him   140
Windmills   29
Wing   35